West Germany

8

‡‡‡‡‡‡‡‡‡‡‡‡‡ *National Planning Series* ‡‡‡‡‡‡‡‡‡‡‡‡‡
BERTRAM M. GROSS, GENERAL EDITOR
‡‡

HANS-JOACHIM ARNDT, presently a management consultant to various institutions and commercial associations in West Germany, has also served as public relations adviser to the West German affiliate of Standard Oil, chief of the economic bureau of the Free Democratic party in Bonn, and as research affiliate to a West German bank.

Arndt is author of five other volumes in the fields of sociology, political science, and business management, and a number of his articles and speeches have been published.

He is the holder of the M.A. degree from Washington University, St. Louis, Missouri, and the Ph.D. degree from the University of Heidelberg. He has also served as fellow in the Graduate School of Public Administration, Harvard University, lecturer in the University of Heidelberg, and member of the third cycle of the Fondation des Sciences Politiques in Paris.

West Germany
Politics of Non-Planning

HANS-JOACHIM ARNDT

Preface by

BERTRAM M. GROSS

SYRACUSE UNIVERSITY PRESS

Acknowledgment

This and other volumes in the National Planning
Series were initiated with the encouragement and
support of Stephen K. Bailey, Dean of the Maxwell
Graduate School of Citizenship and Public Affairs,
Syracuse University, and of his predecessor, Harlan
Cleveland. They have been made possible through a
grant from the Ford Foundation for cross-cultural
research by the Maxwell School. Nora F. Gross de-
serves recognition for her invaluable assistance in
editing the manuscript. The efforts of Lambert
Wenner in the final editing are also appreciated.

BERTRAM M. GROSS

Manufactured in the United States of America

‡‡

Acknowledgments

The author wishes to express his gratitude to the Gesellschaft zur Förderung des Unternehmernachwuchses, Cologne, for supplying secretarial facilities, and to Miss Plate, for assistance and help. In no way does this discharge the author from his full responsibility for all factual, logical, and structural errors, and especially for the selective principles, frame of reference, and basic assumptions of this study. None of these can in any way be attributed to the political philosophy of any group inside or outside the German Federal Republic. The collection of material was completed in 1964, with minor additions following the course of events as late as mid-1966.

August 2, 1966   HANS-JOACHIM ARNDT
Rösrath, West Germany

Contents

‡‡‡

The Non-Miracle of German Economic Growth

One of the historic phenomena of the mid-twentieth century—the full meaning of which is still beyond our comprehension—has been the rebirth of Germany and Japan from the devastation of World War II.

In the bloody springtime of 1945, as Allied forces prepared for their last crushing blows in Europe and the Pacific, the Berlin Philharmonic Orchestra in its last concert before evacuation from the smoking city played Wagner's *Die Götterdämmerung,* the Twilight of the Gods. The majestic, funereal music announced the destruction of Valhalla, the death of the gods, and the end of the world.[1] A few weeks later, with the cities of Germany in smoking ruins, the Nazi armies surrendered. A few months later, with Tokyo in flames and the world still quivering in the wake of atomic bombs dropped on Hiroshima and Nagasaki, the Japanese armies surrendered. The fascist Valhalla of the militarists in both countries was indeed destroyed.

Today, both countries have gone far beyond "reconstruction" and have become outstanding examples of burgeoning prosperity and growth. As the only industrially developed nation in Asia, Japan has surpassed all other industrialized nations in its high annual growth rates and is beginning to achieve world-wide leadership in various aspects of high technology production. West Germany—despite partition—is now, as Andrew Shonfield has pointed out, "the most dynamic industrial state in Western Europe."[2] By

[1] The story of this last concert is graphically told in Cornelius Ryan, *The Last Battle* (New York: Simon and Shuster, 1966), pp. 173–76.

[2] Andrew Shonfield, *Modern Capitalism* (New York and London: Oxford

1975, according to Bruce M. Russett's cautious estimates, West Germany will be second only to the United States in material wealth, and Japan's per capita GNP will be far above the European average of the 1950's.[3]

How has all this come about in such a relatively brief period? "Miracles!" This is the superficial, quick answer of many commentators. It is also the answer indirectly suggested by the economic analysts, both German and Japanese, who have either boasted of or complained about the lack of government guidance of growth processes in these countries. In Germany—as in the United States —the official ideology has been opposed to economic planning by central government. Indeed, Ludwig Erhard, first as Minister of Economics and then as Chancellor, has managed to become a living, talking, walking symbol of "non-planning" and old-fashioned, albeit "neoliberal," market economics. The Economic Planning Agency of Japan, along with many similar bodies throughout the world, had become—in the words of Shigeto Tsuru—a symbol of "formal planning divorced from action."[4]

If social scientists, administrators, and national leaders are to equip themselves with the knowledge and skills needed for more successful guidance of significant change in the modern world, it is essential—in my judgment—that we learn much more about the realities of economic growth in Germany and Japan. Both of these countries obtained huge amounts of foreign aid and advice from the countries that had conquered and occupied them. But, unlike many other recipients of foreign assistance, they used such assistance superbly. Today, they are, in turn, giving increasing assistance to other countries recently embarked on the industrializing process in many parts of the world. Moreover, each of them has achieved the economic and technological potential of becoming

University Press, 1965), p. 239. Details on West German growth rates with respect to total and per capita, GNP, output per man-hour, exports, and other economic indicators—in comparison with other Western countries—are provided in Angus Maddison, *Economic Growth in the West* (New York: Twentieth Century Fund, 1964), pp. 25–42.

[3] Bruce M. Russett, *Trends in World Politics* (New York: Macmillan, 1965), pp. 109–16; and Bruce M. Russett et al., *World Handbook of Political and Social Indicators* (New Haven: Yale University Press, 1964), pp. 341–64.

[4] Shigeto Tsuru, "Formal Planning Divorced from Action: Japan," Everett E. Hagen, ed., *Planning Economic Development* (Homewood: Irwin, 1963), pp. 119–49.

once again an important military power—with Germany having already gone much further in this direction than Japan. An understanding of growth processes in each may even throw some light on the persistent question that people in many other countries cannot help but ask: "With the growing economic power of Germany and Japan, is there any danger of a successful rebirth of German or Japanese militarism and aggression?"

While Hans-Joachim Arndt has not addressed himself to this last question, his study of economic practice and policy in West Germany may be hopefully regarded as a forerunner of a "new style" in the scientific study of countries like Germany and Japan. Dr. Arndt has provided the first detailed analysis yet available in English of the economic measures undertaken in recent years by the West German government (Chapter II). He has placed this picture in the broader perspective of the failures of the Weimar Republic, the "memories of planned scarcity as practiced by the reactionary Nazi regime," and the "bitter experiences of East Germany" under highly centralized planning (Chapter I). He has carefully—and impertinently as well as pertinently—dissected the prevailing "neoliberal" and "social market" ideologies. Too realistic to be shocked by the sharp differences between ideology and practice, he has pointed out the "practical importance" of theoretical debates (Chapter III). Completely at home in the world of economic measures and policies, he has penetrated "behind the scenes" and helped us understand the more human and meaningful world of men and their motives (Chapter IV), of groups and their policies (Chapter V). In his "preliminary appraisal" he makes it very clear that "macroeconomic planning is not a technological but a political issue" (p. 121). He makes this comment not in order to foreclose discussion of the political issue (as most economists seem to do) but to open up for even deeper discussion the entire subject of the "politics of non-planning" and the "politics of planning" (Chapter VI). It would indeed be a fruitful service to both "academics" and "practical men" if Dr. Arndt, while continuing and deepening his analysis of Germany, were also to compare Japanese with German growth and Japanese with German political leaders. In Japan, Prime Minister Shigeru Yoshida was in many ways similar to Chancellor Erhard. For him also "the word 'planning' was anathema." Yet in 1956 Yoshida was succeeded by Prime Minister

Nobusuke Kishi, who immediately produced a "New Long-Range Economic Plan" and then in 1960 by Prime Minister Hayato Ikeda, who produced a still more ambitious plan under the slogan "Double Your Income in Ten Years!"[5] What are the probabilities that Erhard might be succeeded by a German version of Kishi or Ikeda?

The careful reader of Dr. Arndt's study, however, cannot fail to be concerned with many basic questions, some raised explicitly by Arndt, some derived from the very nature of his subject matter. Those involved in the comparative study of "system guidance" in many different kinds of national systems will be particularly concerned with such matters as

(1) the nature of real-life planning, as distinguished from slogans;
(2) the implications of "generational intermingling" at the top levels of government and of private organizations; and
(3) the relation between economic expansion and military power in the "advanced" societies.

Let us take a brief look at each of these separately, with particular attention to their implications for the future.

ANTI-PLANNING SLOGANS AND PLANNING REALITIES

As the "mystique" of national economic planning has swept through the pre-industrial world, we have seen one example after another of "façade planning" or "paper planning," with very little being done to carry out the brave new plans. Douglas E. Ashford has suggested that before genuine planning for industrialization can get underway in some pre-industrial societies, it may be necessary to go through a transitional stage of symbolic or ritualistic planning. "Symbolic planning occurs when preplanning attitudes develop as a convenient psychological adjustment to avoid changing behavior. Ritualistic planning occurs when behavior is actually changed in specific ways without being backed by attitudinal adjustments. . . . Symbolic planning is strengthened by changed behavior, whereas ritualistic planning is strengthened by changed attitudes."[6]

[5] *Ibid.*
[6] Bertram M. Gross, "From Symbolism to Action," Prefatory Comment to

In some of these countries, indeed, the oratory of symbolic and ritualistic planning has died down and effective, action-oriented planning institutions and processes have come into being. In Mexico, as revealed by Robert J. Shafer, this has happened without the symbolic creation of a single, highly visible central planning agency. Hence commentators and scholars who are more impressed by symbols than facts may conclude that Mexico—whose national economic planning is more effective and sophisticated than that of any other Latin American country with the possible exception of Venezuela—is a country without national planning.[7]

In contrast, there are the two giants of Western industrialism, the United States and West Germany. Here the prevailing symbols and rituals at the level of central government have been those of "non-planning" or even "anti-planning." These symbols and rituals are closely associated with deeply embedded doctrines and ideologies of private enterprise and market competition. In the United States, both before and after World War II, it became *de rigueur* that any political leaders or government officials advocating more government planning justify their measures as steps to strengthen private enterprise and market competition. Thus many American commentators have observed that "if socialism ever comes to America, it will come in the name of free enterprise." This is a variant of the older, and rather terrifying, statement of the Louisiana politician Huey Long that "if fascism ever comes to America, it will come in the name of democracy." The juxtaposition of these two statements and the one in the text should not be regarded as suggesting any similarity between socialism and fascism, but rather as pointing to the "change logic" of using symbols of the past to justify something entirely different in the future. Indeed, another variation—highly applicable to the Communist countries in Eastern Europe—would be the proposition that "If market competition ever comes to Russia and her Communist neighbors, it will come in the name of socialism." Thus the leading Polish economist and planner, Oskar Lange, shortly before his death, argued that tight central control was not genuine socialism. The new socialist society "matures," he wrote,

Douglas E. Ashford, *Morocco-Tunisia: Politics and Planning* (Syracuse: Syracuse University Press, 1965), p. viii.

[7] Robert J. Shafer, *Mexico: Mutual Adjustment Planning* (Syracuse: Syracuse University Press, 1966).

only at the moment when it "starts to overcome these centralistic, bureaucratic methods of administrative planning."[8]

In the United States, one of the many reasons for the strength of "non-planning" and "anti-planning" symbols has been the fabulous strength and spread of "subsystem planning." Between World War I and World War II large private corporations developed hitherto undreamed-of capacities to formulate and carry out long-range plans for the production and marketing of goods. After World War II, with a host of new managerial techniques for planning and control and with a new world of science and technology opened up by the great advances in information processing, electronics, and chemistry the capacities of these huge subsystems rose to qualitatively higher level. At the same time various specialized government agencies—particularly those operating in national defense, outer space, air transport, and public roads—reached comparable levels of effectiveness. Pressures for central national planning or coordination were counteracted in the following ways by the planned operations of these private and public giants:

(1) Their success in meeting human needs through limited, special-purpose planning created conditions under which the need for central coordination or guidance has been something less than compelling; and

(2) The power of these subsystems constituted tremendous forces of resistance to any efforts toward imposing strong central controls upon them.

On the other hand, the successes of subsystem planning have also created certain tendencies leading toward the development of new forms of central guidance:

(1) American elites have become increasingly "planning minded," and the first thing a modern-style corporation executive usually does upon entering government service is to initiate a more sophisticated system of planning in his own agency;

(2) As subsystem planning becomes increasingly complex,

---

[8] Oskar Lange, *On Functioning of the Socialist Economy,* Part I, Volume 23 of The Advanced Course in National Economic Planning (Warsaw, 1965), mimeo, p. 38.

many problems are faced that can *only* be handled through some sort of cross-sectoral or truly national decision-making activity; and

(3) New ways have been found (many of them informal and "behind the scenes") for the "central guidance cluster" to bring major subsystems, private and public, into the central planning process without their giving up much of their highly prized power or any of their still more highly prized status and prestige.

Accordingly, we have already entered a period in the United States during which "planning" and "programing" at the highest levels of government is being converted from anathema to religion. By 1963 and 1964 the allegedly "new" conservative Keynesian economics had already been translated into tax cuts that boosted output, income, and employment. In 1965 President Johnson announced a new national planning system which, while concentrating upon the planning of government's expanding operations, was also intimately tied in with planned actions to affect nongovernmental operations. If he had called it a "Planning System" alone, the semantics of his announcement might have caused raised eyebrows and a wave of alarm. As it was, he set up something much more powerful—not just a planning system, but a system for crystallizing plans into detailed programs and backing up programs with the resources provided by detailed budgets. Thus at an historic Cabinet meeting in August, 1965, President Johnson announced his new "Planning-Programing-Budgeting System," based upon the "systems analysis" planning developed some years earlier by Secretary McNamara at the Department of Defense. Since then, while the old symbols still have meaning, "planning" has been emerging as the new mystique of American government.

In West Germany also, as Dr. Arndt has pointed out, there has been a vast amount of government intervention and guidance in economic affairs—despite the "non-planning" slogans. His judgment is supported by other commentators. Thus Angus Maddison has discussed the so-called German "miracle" in the following terms:

There is a tendency to discount the role of policy in Germany and exaggerate the economic "miracle." This is partly because the Minister of Economics, Dr. Erhard, was wont to expound

German policy in simplified terms, and partly because the
techniques of policy were different from those used in the
slow-growing countries. However, the German authorities followed a vigorous line of action in each of the three major
aspects of growth policy: management of demand, maintenance of competitiveness, and fostering output potential by
policies fostering high investment and foreign trade.[9]

In his brilliant comparative survey of European and American
capitalism, Andrew Shonfield has gone even further in deflating
the myths of German "non-planning." Indeed, he goes so far as to
suggest that, without the elaborate paraphernalia of consultative
committees and formal plan documents, the Germans have been
doing at least as much national economic planning during the past
twenty years as the French.

The Ministry of Economics was most actively intervening
wherever opportunities for more production, aided by strategi-
cally placed subsidies or tax concessions, presented themselves.
Rarely can a ministry so vociferously devoted to the virtues of
economic liberalism and market forces have taken so vigorous
a part in setting the direction and selecting the targets of economic development. . . . When the German government inter-
vened to accelerate the growth of certain sectors of the economy, it went to great lengths to present the matter, wherever it
was possible to do so, as if it derived from or supplemented
some primary private initiative, whereas in France the natural
tendency was, and is, to insist on the public character of such
initiative. Indeed, the German Government seemed at times
almost to be trying to disguise what it was doing even from
itself. . . .[10] Thus, the German Government set up a series of
targets for economic recovery—basic industries, exports, housing—and concentrated the resources of the nation on them,

---

[9] Maddison, *Economic Growth in the West* (New York: Twentieth Century
Fund, 1964), p. 102. Maddison maintains that there was in Germany, in fact,
despite the anti-planning philosophy of the social market economy, "a fiscal policy which provided stronger investment incentives than in most countries. While
no target of potential growth was set forth, there was a very careful attempt to
promote demand, and in the latter part of the 1950's this policy was pushed to
the limit the economy could stand without inflation." pp. 151–52.

[10] Shonfield, *Modern Capitalism,* p. 275.

one after another. Public saving, combined with the great ploughback of profits by firms fed on tax concessions, provided the finances for these extensive investments. . . .[11]

One of the reasons the German government has been effective with these measures is the growth and strength, as in America, of subsystem planning by business enterprises. As Dr. Arndt explains, this involves not only "microeconomic planning" but also extensive cooperation among firms and branches. Above all, there is what Arndt calls the "unique structure" of German banking. Arndt's extensive writings on this subject are not yet translated into English, but Andrew Shonfield, too, has gone into considerable detail in spelling out the promotional and coordinating roles of the "Big Three" in German banking. "The big banks," he suggests, "have always seen it as their business to take an overall view of the long-term trend in any industry in which they were concerned, and then to press individual firms to conform to certain broad lines of development."[12] In this process a major role is also played by the branch and national industrial associations—with both bankers and association personnel working in close and continuous contact with government officialdom.[13] Indeed, with all the reports on the enormous physical destruction caused by the World War II bombing of Germany, it should be kept in mind that the Nazi regime was the only major *institution* that was destroyed. The business, banking, and industrial institutions—modified to some extent by the anticartel laws—remained in existence. Together with the formidable bureaucracy of the government agencies, they provided the institutional underpinnings of reconstruction and guided expansion.

Unlike United States economic policy statements, German postwar statements were inevitably affected by the inescapable influence of the occupation authorities, particularly by the United States. Indeed, a considerable part of the "non-planning" orientation of the Germans probably derived from an effort to make statements that would sound acceptable to American ears and contribute to the maintenance of a large in-flow of American aid. Today, however, this situation has changed. West Germany is better able to

---

[11] *Ibid.*, p. 283.
[12] *Ibid.*, p. 261.
[13] *Ibid.*, pp. 239–64.

stand on its own feet. The United States, still a partner (if not mentor) of West Germany, is committed to national planning in terms that are becoming increasingly explicit. Accordingly, it becomes increasingly likely that Erhard may in fact be succeeded by a Yoshida or a Kishi. Indeed, he might yet himself become an explicit advocate of German-style national planning—if not to "double income in 10 years," then to usher in the glories of the "Formierte Gesellschaft."

GENERATIONAL INTERMINGLING

One of Dr. Arndt's great contributions to the literature of national planning is that, rather than confining himself to the formal structure of government, he has given us a panoramic picture of major subsystems in German society. As Joseph LaPalombara has done with Italian planning,[14] he has identified the posture of major interest groups in West Germany. The keenness of his observations and his willingness to write directly and to the point are illustrated —to mention but one of many examples—by his description of how interest group representatives infiltrate the civil service after being labeled "experts." But then, Arndt observes, " 'expertism' did not need to be introduced into government via interest groups; *it could be bought at universities and was called jurisprudence*" (p. 64, Editor's italics).

Going much further than LaPalombara, however, Dr. Arndt has initiated a stimulating and impressive form of social psychological inquiry into certain shared attitudes and values of different generations. While touching upon various age groups among politicians and labor leaders, he concentrates upon the group with which he has had the most intimate contact, namely, businessmen. Here he suggests certain broad differences among three groups: the "grandfathers," the "grandsons," and the in-between group of the "sons."

The "grandfathers," according to Dr. Arndt, are those who

(1) not only lived through World War I but also "navigated through the Nazi period, cooperating as necessary with politicians and immoral elements in order to keep their business afloat" (p. 57);

14 Joseph LaPalombara, *Italy: The Politics of Planning* (Syracuse: Syracuse University Press, 1966).

(2) were the dominant elements in the expansion of German
business, at least until 1963 (p. 57); and

(3) "accept the political myths of nation, state, fatherland,
and people and their representatives, with no intermediary agents such as interest groups, ministries or political
parties" (p. 51).

The "sons," in sharp contrast,

(1) are still shaken by the radical changes they have experienced in their lifetime, expecting treachery of all sorts
(p. 52);

(2) shun risks or great responsibilities, preferring the "survival first" attitude of *nous, après le deluge* (p. 53); and

(3) are skeptical of technical tricks (p. 53).

The "grandsons," in turn,

(1) like the grandfathers, not only resist change but cannot
conceive of fundamental change, (p. 52);

(2) unlike the grandfathers, participate actively in "practical
party and pressure group work," particularly at the level
of the local diets and Länder parliaments (p. 52), and

(3) unlike the fathers, believe they can transfer to politics
"the skill, knowledge and techniques as learned and applied in business practice" (p. 53).

Insofar as West Germany is concerned, one may hope that this
kind of analysis may be, in time, carried much further. What, for
example, are the generational differences in German universities?
How many social scientists with the originality and profundity of a
Hans-Joachim Arndt are on German faculties? How many such as
he are coming up from the ranks of present-day graduate students?

Still more broadly, however, the question of generational intermingling goes to the very heart of a nation's social structure, internal conflicts, and all efforts to plan for the future. While generational conflict has always been a part of life, a distinguishing characteristic of the modern world is longer life expectancy and, with
the miracles of modern medicine and living standards, greater expectations on the part of older people to play vigorous, active, and
even creative roles after fifty, sixty, and seventy. This might be

called "activity expectancy." Chronological age is less and less a determinant of mental (or even physical) vigor. Hence there are (and will probably increasingly be) more and more older people actively taking part in social activity, side by side with many younger generations. Probably still more important is the rapid rate of technological and social change. This means many new "critical change points" in every lifetime, creating more frequent problems of personal adjustment, threatening more people with obsolescence unless they learn new skills and attitudes, and opening up the opportunities for "many careers in one lifetime." The result of all this is that in "social time" generational differences occur much more quickly than ever before. While some of us may still think of three coexisting generations in "family-life time," we also observe that the successive generations of university students must be divided into groups of not longer (and perhaps much shorter) than a decade. Indeed, we are entering a period of intermingling and conflict among at least six generations of people with different values, interests, and attitudes. These complex inter-generational conflicts must invariably leave an important imprint upon plans and planners.

ECONOMIC GROWTH AND MILITARY EXPANSION

Students of national planning must indeed work hard to insulate themselves from recurring questions concerning the relation of their subject matter to war preparations, militarism, and warfare. Historically, armies and general staffs were the first large-scale organizations to engage in the long-range planning of large-scale operations. In industrial societies, such planning cannot be insulated from economic activities in general. It requires a firm economic base in such sectors as manufacturing, transportation, communication, and finance. In the present age of nuclear, bacteriological, chemical, and outer space defense systems, it requires long-range planning associated with a country's major activities on the frontiers of science and technology.

As Dr. Arndt has pointed out, the bitter memory of the Nazis' wartime economic planning is one of the factors tending to make the very idea of national planning unpalatable in West Germany. In the United States, also, it should be recalled that the end of World War II brought a deep emotional revulsion against the controls that had been imposed under wartime central planning and a vigorous program of "decontrol." Indeed, with the coming of the Korean war in 1950, even the most vigorous advocates of "remobilization" were very wary against an over-tightening of central planning measures. In Japan the pro-planning Prime Ministers and Cabinets that came into power immediately after the war did not last very long. The anti-planning bias of the Yoshida government that came into power in 1949 certainly derived support from memories of wartime regimentation as well as from the laissez faire ideology of U.S. occupation authorities.

Today, however, wartime memory is less significant. For one thing, there is a large new generation of younger people who remember little or nothing of the wartime period. More important, it is now becoming clear that national planning by central governments does not necessarily involve detailed control. The latest technologies of economic planning emphasize extensive use of price systems, market mechanisms, decentralized government, and widespread participation in planning processes. The experiences of many countries show that increased national planning need be no threat to political democracy. Indeed, improved national planning—which can rarely be effective without significant government decentralization and the promotion of regulated markets—may in some countries constitute a major contribution toward more democratic forms of decision-making. Under these circumstances the connection between war and planning becomes a much *more,* not less, important question.

I gravely doubt, however, whether this question can be properly approached within the narrow perspective of whether or not Germany or Japan, with their vast economic potentials, will once again become great military powers. Political decision-making in these countries takes place within the framework of a world society which subjects them to new and difficult pressures. Thus it is the United States—probably much more than any group of West German leaders—that has pushed the Germans into limited (albeit nonnuclear) rearmament and an ever-greater role in the NATO military forces. In turn, the foreign policies of the Soviet Union have had an unmistakable effect upon U.S. policies and West German rearmament. The testing of nuclear bombs by Communist China has already created a situation in which the Japanese may soon reconsider their past resistance to rearmament. Beyond this, and without detracting attention from the specifics of military planning in West Germany and Japan, I suggest that new attention be given to one of the great problems of the coming decades: namely, *the possibility that successfully planned economic growth may lead a nation into activities of domination, if not aggression, beyond its borders.*

This possibility has been vigorously presented by one of the world's most cautious and objective economic analysts, Simon Kuznetz. In an essay entitled "Toward a Theory of Economic Growth," Kuznetz presents these disturbing observations:

> Rapid economic growth of a country, once it is of a certain size, seems to be associated with extensive expansion (which often means aggression) or with the exertion of pressure on other reluctant nations to accept changes desirable to it. Great Britain, the rapidly growing economic leader in the late eighteenth and through most of the nineteenth century, thus expended its power and enforced a Pax Britannica through much of the world. The United States extended its territory by purchase or by minor wars in the nineteenth century, opened up Japan by the Perry mission, and acquired control over the Philippines. Japan, once opened up, displayed aggressive tendencies through much of its modern history. Germany used wars as stepping stones to further expansion. This association does not mean that aggressive elements exist only in external relations of sizable countries experiencing rapid economic growth; they easily arise out of other conditions. But there do seem to be some almost compulsive factors in a rapidly growing country, provided it is of some minimum size, to display aggressive elements in its external relations with others. . . . Rapid growth is evidence of success which lends assurance to the country and its leaders that their economic and social practices have proved right, that their views on organizing society for economic functions have met the test of success, and that if adopted in other countries, they would be equally successful. Further, this success persuades them that they have a responsibility to widen the scope of this successful type of economic organization, to urge adoption of some of its basic

features by those countries that have not been successful and for their eventual benefit.[15]

Although Kuznetz makes it perfectly clear that there are many other causes of war and that tendencies toward foreign expansiveness need not always result in war, his analysis broadens the framework for considering the dangers inherent in the new economic power of West Germany and Japan. If we follow his suggestion, we must consider the dangers inherent in planned economic growth throughout the world—in the United States as well as in the Soviet Union, Israel, and Egypt,[16] and in India and Pakistan as well as Communist China. It is highly dangerous to accept the modern, Western version of economic determinism which holds that economic growth is an antidote to war. It is more realistic—and of greater service to human interests—to recognize the dangers inherent in nationalistic planning and the urgent need for social scientists to give more attention to the possibilities of transnational planning for world peace.

BERTRAM M. GROSS

Syracuse, New York
Fall 1966

[15] Simon Kuznetz, *Economic Growth and Structure, Selected Essays* (New York: Norton, 1965), pp. 49, 51.
[16] This point is developed in "War and Economic Development," the concluding section in my preface to Benjamin Akzin and Yehezkel Dror, *Israel: High-Pressure Planning* (Syracuse: Syracuse University Press, 1966), pp. xxviii–xxxii.

Historical Roots and Reasons

The scholar who assumes the task of studying national economic planning in West Germany today touches immediately upon a political taboo. The first German experience with governmental planning was with rationing and allocations during World War I, under Kaiser Wilhelm. The German people, moreover, have vivid memories of planned scarcity as practiced by the National Socialist regime. Furthermore, their judgment of the evils of planning in the Soviet Union has been reinforced by what they know of the bitter experiences of East Germany. Planning has been so thoroughly debunked politically that even its former advocates look for new words, sometimes new forms, to replace it. If a study on economic planning can, nevertheless, serve any purpose for a society which abhors the very sound of the word, it may be this: to reveal the dividing line that can be drawn between formal "highly centralized planning," on the one hand, and a "loosely planned market economy" on the other.

THE WEIMAR REPUBLIC

Germany's first democratic regime, the Weimar Republic, was formed at a time of utter political and military disaster and faced the prospect of almost complete economic, financial, and social disintegration. Its stabilizer was the Social Democratic party, by tradition one of the best organized and strongest socialist parties in Europe. But since the Republic was also supported by more conservative elements, it is not astonishing to learn that its internal domestic life was a continuous struggle between conservatives and the advocates of planning on the left.

1

The Weimar Republic, though relatively short lived, left an indelible mark: some of its accomplishments and even some of its slogans have survived the National Socialist and postwar periods. The Weimar heritage, moreover, is responsible for some of the economic thinking in present-day Germany.[1]

The first phase of the Republic, from 1919 to the currency reform of 1923, went from uncertainty, through ill-digested and disorganized experiment, to monetary chaos. The Social Democratic party, which had had a mass base of all the left-wing elements, was deserted at first by the Independent Socialists, then by the Communists, and finally was left with the moderate "liberal" Socialists. These assumed responsibility both for the presidency (Reich President Friedrich Ebert, until 1925) and for the government (as head or part of the "Weimar coalition"), but they had no clearly defined program or even a concept of how to organize one.

The Communists were no better off. They could not yet commit themselves to a regime of workers', soldiers', and peasants' councils. Moreover, their model—Soviet Russia—had just turned from Lenin's War Communism (based on what he knew of the recently ended German War Economy) to his New Economic Policy (NEP), a limited, controlled market.[2] New economic plan designers were nowhere evident.

The German Social Democrats, so recently identical with the Communists, were in substantially the same position as the Russians except that, having come to power in a more developed country and at a time of financial ruin, they were prudent enough not to damage the economy still further by excessive and untimely experimenting. While Socialists, labor union leaders, and intellectuals talked a lot, the practical results were negligible. The so-called Economic Parliament,[3] for example, was completely ineffectual, but some of the experimental planning actions did last for a longer time: the Workers Councils in Enterprise, set up under a law passed in 1920 and revised in 1952; a system giving special protection to tenants against landlords, started in 1923 and lifted only partially in 1960;[4] a government-sponsored cartel for coal and potash, which lasted until the end of World War II;[5] and the establishment and safeguarding of the eight-hour day and the right of collective bargaining.

But despite these partial and haphazard attempts to regulate economic action, the German economy turned almost automatically to market liberalism. Paradoxically enough, this is affirmed by the runaway inflation which developed in the course of the period under review. It was due to laissez faire principles that an adminis- trative measure—the extraordinary expansion of paper money— was allowed to exert its full influence on prices and market and that speculators were allowed to take in the heavy gains produced by the destruction of the currency system.

The currency reform of 1923–24, which finally ended this tragedy, was neither a product of the normal market mechanism nor the result of normal parliamentary procedures. New adminis- trative measures were enacted October 12, 1923, after parliament had emasculated itself by passing a law declaring a state of emer- gency, suspending the Civil Rights Charter of the Constitution, and transferring supreme power to the executive. Hjalmar Schacht, cer- tainly not a leftist planner, was made Reich Commissar of Currency and later became president of the Central Bank. It was he who then initiated the swing toward "business." The right wing around Karl Helfferich took credit for the enactment and success of the currency reform, although the emergency law was passed with the help of the Social Democrats *against* the right-wing members of the Reichs- tag. For the prosperous years to come, the Socialists had voted themselves out of power. Their name became linked with the ex- perimental years starting with revolution and ending with currency reform.

The middle class, contrary to the belief of the orthodox Marxists in the Socialist party, would probably have normally served as the mass base for the Social Democratic party, which, having split from Communism, was making attempts to become "liberal," "honest," and "acceptable" to the center wing.[6] But the middle class had lost its savings, was no longer economically stable, and was subject to left-wing attack in any crisis.

The currency reform ushered in a four-year period of high income and employment, peace and normalcy. From 1924 to 1928 Germany was governed by a succession of coalition cabinets based on the three bourgeois, moderately nationalistic parties: Catholic Center party, the Democrats (liberal), and the People's party

(Stresemann's). In the memory of many, this "good life period" of Weimar is connected with the restoration of an unplanned economy operating with a reformed currency.

The underlying trend of this time was "free market" liberalism based upon domestic labor and foreign money, with the questions of reparations and occupation slowly becoming negotiable. Only two major acts of government intervention can be identified with this middle period of the Weimar Republic. They proved lasting.

The first was an extension of state arbitration in labor disputes. Compulsory arbitration of wage conflicts was enacted in 1927 by a coalition of center and right-of-center parties. This law was used by the National Socialists in 1934 for their own purposes but was repealed after the Allied victory in 1945. Today, the issue is still a critical one between management and labor, who threaten each other with reintroducing a system to control the other's freedom of action.

The second piece of social legislation was unemployment insurance. It became a turning point of politics. Closely connected with economic liberalism, this system used classical insurance methods. But it was equally involved in efforts to overcome involuntary idleness by the intervention through macroeconomic fiscal policies. It was certainly more than just historical irony that a fight over the amount of unemployment compensation caused the breakdown of the last functioning Weimar coalition in 1930.

In 1928 a center-to-left coalition had replaced the bourgeois government, but it could not survive the strain and stress of the Great Depression, one of the greatest economic crises in world history. By 1929, its first signs were apparent. In the end of that year the budget of the federal government showed a deficit of 1.7 billion marks. The Minister of Finance resigned, as did the Central Bank president. On March 27, 1930, the coalition government headed by Social Democrat Chancellor Hermann Müller broke up.

A succession of new government heads tried various orthodox and unorthodox methods to restore the German economy, mainly deflationary or inflationary measures which served to curtail or to extend the income of particular groups. Macroeconomic control was unknown; Keynes in Great Britain, and Föhl and Nöll von der Nahmer in Germany, had not yet published their "New Economics."[7]

What followed was a regime by presidential decrees, ignoring a parliament paralyzed by radical minorities from left and right. One of the last decrees of this sort was the nomination of Adolf Hitler to the chancellery. Neither the moderate left-wing nor the moderate right-wing partisans of today have ever forgotten the helplessness of the Weimar authorities when they were confronted with the grave economic disorders of this period. Their actual political thinking seems to be determined more by this retrospective judgment of Weimar than by their present evaluation of Bonn. Some argue that a depression such as that of 1929 can be easily avoided today by using modern instruments of economic control that do not fully break with market economy principles. Others feel that only limited planning is sufficient to avoid such economic disaster.

Hence, in economics as well as in politics the period of Weimar still represents a part of the uncomprehended past. There is a slight tendency, however, to oversimplify the picture and to argue that just as in politics the Weimar party strife was more tolerable than the Nazi concentration camps and World War II, so economically the Great Depression itself was more tolerable than total war destruction and postwar chaos. Hence, so the argument runs, if we believe only a little bit in the increased capacity of our economists to avert the worst crises with methods that do not damage the market, the future will be safe through economic liberalism.

After all, the only happy period through which the Germans lived between the outbreak of World War I and World War II was the four years of mid-Weimar, 1924 to 1928. And at that time Germany had a coalition government somewhat similar to that which established stability from 1949 to 1964, and there was an economic policy and economic development not unlike that of the present time. Had there also been, in the twenties, the international trade and Western unity of today, instead of financial disequilibrium caused by unrealistic reparation and war debt claims, Weimar might have been permanent. So popular judgment runs.

THE THIRD REICH AND ITS AFTERMATH

Shortly before coming to power in 1933, Hitler asked Reich Central Bank President Luther (who had assumed office on

Schacht's resignation in 1930) how much money the Reichsbank
could provide to put the six million unemployed back to work.
Luther is said to have answered, "150 million Reichsmark."
(Unemployment relief in 1932 already amounted to three billion
Reichsmark.) Schacht, when asked the same question, replied,
"As much as will prove necessary."[8]

It was Schacht who was renamed bank president in 1933 and
appointed Minister of Economics in 1934. By introducing an unorthodox form of currency (the MEFO bills of exchange) to
finance employment programs, he succeeded in reducing the number of unemployed to four million by the end of 1933 and to two
and six-tenths million by the end of 1934. This was done before
any rearmament measures were put into action by Hitler.[9]

Nöll von der Nahmer, one of the theoretical designers of
Schacht's financial policy, said in 1948, "Monetary theories falsely
interpreted have plunged this world into times of distress beyond
example. The only benefit which can now be drawn out of the world
economic crisis is that these errors can be considered overcome."[10]

The full employment policy of the National Socialists, however,
cannot simply be regarded as a kind of Keynesian deficit spending
avant la lettre. Nor can it be accurately compared to the Roosevelt
New Deal or similar policies pursued by Western democracies to
meet the crisis. Hitler's total design not only deviated from orthodox
financing but also marked a break with all other liberal conceptions
of sound economic and social policy.

First there was discrimination for noneconomic reasons, starting
quite early. On April 1, 1933, a boycott against shops and stores
owned by Jewish citizens was made official. In the same month,
there followed the law banning Jews from the civil service. On
September 15, 1935, the regime proclaimed the Nuremberg Laws
"for protecting German blood and honor" by depriving Jews of
German citizenship. By 1938, the Jews were removed from participation in almost all forms of economic activity.

But the greatest ideological strength of the National Socialists
lay in the fight against economic liberalism, a fight that had been
proclaimed in the party platform and was supported by many who
did not go along with most of the other Nazi aims in politics, economics, and ideology. Moreover, in the German middle class there
was a widespread dislike of commercialism and its political aspects:

economic liberalism, capitalism, the market economy, and world trade. This "anticapitalist desire" (*antikapitalistische Sehnsucht*) was expressed through youth movements and "conservative revolutionaries"[11] of all types. Even Hjalmar Schacht, the acting president of the Central Bank, as far back as the mid-twenties attacked the "cash-nexus-society" as inhuman.[12]

The National Socialist economic policy makers after 1933 could therefore expect rather widespread acclaim when they started to remodel society according to some version of a corporate state. In this effort, they used as standards various aspects of Italian fascism, guild socialism, and their own mixture of private cartels and state guidance. Private property remained guaranteed but was directed, in accordance with the slogan "Commonweal before private benefit" (*Gemeinnutz geht vor Eigennutz*), into the service of the state party.

In the last analysis, however, National Socialist economic policy was not an outflow of anticapitalist romanticism but an application of technocratic rules. It was not the party ideologue Gottfried Feder or the "universalistic" Professor Othmar Spann who designed economic policy, but men like Schacht and, later, Speer. At any rate, the second German "planned economy" was, like the first one, not introduced by left-wing partisans but came from the right. This must be remembered when the historical impact of these experiences is discussed.

Deliberalization of the economy developed slowly. The full employment measures mentioned were still put to work with the active help of entrepreneurs. During the first years of the Third Reich, economic and social policy aimed for a regulated economy (*gelenkte Wirtschaft*) as an instrument rather than for a planned economy (*Planwirtschaft*) as a target. "Businessmen help to regulate" (*Unternehmer lenken mit*) was the slogan which lured and attracted the support of many a tycoon.

The declared aims of economic policy were, at first, full employment and autarky (self-sufficiency with respect to foreign trade). The business community cooperated with little reservation in this first phase of economic reconstruction. "Its political activity was, in reality, the continuation of business practice by other means."[13] For example, a decree on the organization of stockholding companies (*Aktiengesetz*) of January 30, 1937, restricted the shareholders' powers and transferred special privileges to executive boards. Incidentally, this law was valid until 1965.

The "partners" of business, the trade unions, with their political friends, the Socialists, were treated quite differently. By May, 1933, all trade unions with the exception of the National Socialist Shop Steward Organization (NSBO) were dissolved by decree. Their membership was transferred to the new official "German Workers' Front" (*Deutsche Arbeitsfront*). The law to regulate national labor (*Gesetz zur Ordnung der Nationalen Arbeit*)[14] organized the relations between management and labor through a mixture of business leadership and interference by the state.

In September, 1936, planning was introduced with a Four-Year Plan, and Reichsmarshal Herman Göring was named administrator. The proclaimed targets of the plan were: regulation of basic production, import-export control, allocation of basic resources, regulation of orders and credit, price control, and strengthening the control of foreign exchange. But, except for a price and wage freeze, little was attempted in the way of a fully planned economy, despite the name borrowed from the Bolshevist foe.

Göring's administration of the Four-Year Plan marked the passing over to an armament race which finally turned the entire economy into a weapons plant.[15] From 1933 to about 1937 there had been a marked increase in employment and of production for private consumption, with prices remaining steady.

On November 24, 1937, Schacht resigned from his post as Minister of Economics but stayed in the cabinet at Hitler's request as Minister without Portfolio and retained the office of president of the Reichsbank. He quit the bank post after an open quarrel with Hitler, on January 20, 1939.[16] This was the time when the earlier idea of helping to regulate the economy could no longer be maintained; war was already in the air. But it was not until well into the war that a fully planned economy went into effect with the establishment of a planning office in October, 1942. The planned economy continued technically to function satisfactorily despite war losses, air raids, and blockades. It allocated the increasingly scarce resources so as to make possible continued production for the war effort and the feeding of a population composed of slave laborers and combatants.

And this is exactly the memory which the German population has of the National Socialist economy—its ability to produce whatever was wanted by its leaders, and the fact that a rising standard of living had never been on the agenda of these leaders. Once again, the memory of a part of the historical past is ambivalent. The system applied was technically efficient, both in creating full employment and in war production, but it never produced or even aimed at what is now, after World War II, regarded as the most important goal of an economy: an affluent society.

There is one more word to add on the lasting results of the National Socialist economic policy; it concerns a memory which may live in the unconscious of contemporaries. Though the experiment was one coming from the right wing, and though it was carried on for at least half of its time as a regulated economy rather than as a planned society, the Germans retain a taste of what a "joint effort" in economic matters really means. A joint economic effort, or any kind of economic cooperation, implies a sociological technique which has to introduce something other than competition as its motivating spirit. One has to rally not only a majority of voters, but an entire people. It may seem easy to rally a people in order to achieve, by economic means, a political aim shared by a vast majority, e.g., full employment. The writer thinks that, had there been a completely free vote in, say, 1936 on the issue of full employment, the economic policy crew of Hitler would have received the 99 per cent backing which Hitler received in the (probably manipulated) Reichstag election on March 29, 1936, after remilitarization of the Rhineland.

However, those who have studied and understood the phenomenon of a "rallied people," which appears to be a prerequisite for centralized economic planning, cannot ignore its implications. It is at least questionable whether the economic cooperation necessary for such planning is possible without undermining political individualism and individual rights.[17]

This is, to reiterate, a lesson which some Germans may keep in their unconscious as a sociological and psychological corollary of a planned economy. The purely economic lesson is remembered in a different way: the last and lasting impression of a planned economy was not of economic chaos but of organized scarcity. The political lesson, a combination of the others, is abetted by the massive distress obviously produced by the planning systems the Germans have had experience with—especially when contrasted with the remarkable success which the liberalist economy has produced in West Germany since 1948.

‡‡‡‡‡‡‡‡‡‡‡‡‡‡‡‡‡‡‡‡‡‡‡‡‡II‡‡‡‡‡‡‡‡‡‡‡‡‡‡‡‡‡‡‡‡‡‡‡‡‡‡‡

After the 1948 Currency Reform

ECONOMIC RELIBERALIZATION

On June 20, 1948, more than one year before the creation of the Federal Republic, a currency reform was initiated through laws issued by the military occupation government. A new monetary unit was introduced, the Deutsche Mark (DM). The ratio to its predecessor was scaled, depending upon the nature of debts, from zero (government debts), 6.5 per cent (savings and cash), 10 per cent (mortgages and other private debts), to 100 per cent (rents, wages, and prices).[1] This devaluation was an official acknowledgment of the inflationary movement prevalent since 1938. Once more the holders of monetary assets were hurt. As in 1923, the middle class suffered.

The currency reform marked the beginning of a series of Allied interventions in the field of economics which followed the de-Nazification, *Ent-Junkerung,* demilitarization, dismantling, and other "de-actions" in the political field. In fact, most of these economic de-actions were linked with antecedent or corresponding political measures which marked them as "de-politizations" (removal of political elements from the economic process) irrespective of whether they were initiated by Allied or West German authorities.

Thus, monetary devaluation went together with the reconstruction of a politically independent Central Bank in 1948.[2] In addition, there were measures with the political motive of destroying economic power: decartelization and decentralization (*Konzern-Entflechtung*). Abolition of price and wage control, of rationing, of allocation, and of artificial exchange rates were all designed to free the economy from all noneconomic constraints.[3]

11

This purification of the economy was initially taken at great political risk; the over-all climate in Western Europe, even including some United States occupation authorities, was left of center.[4] The U.S. high commissioner, General Lucius D. Clay, is said to have answered Erhard on his liberalization proposals: "My advisers tell me they are much opposed to this." Erhard is said to have replied, "Never mind, General, mine are telling me the same thing." The U.S. and British control boards had issued strict orders that their explicit consent had to be obtained before any alteration of fixed prices could take place. Erhard circumvented these decrees by simply abolishing most price and wage controls. Finally, General Clay endorsed the German policy.[5]

Lifting of price and wage controls was fiercely opposed by left-wing parties and their Allied and German partisans. The program received its first serious setback when German labor unions called a general strike protesting Erhard's policy at the end of 1948. Many serious adjustment crises occurred in the course of the first years of reliberalization. Increased unemployment, for example, showed that the full employment of the period before the currency reform had really been disguised unemployment. Foreign trade was disrupted by overimporting before the Korean crisis. But none of these were comparable to the opposition which immediately followed currency reform and the lifting of controls. It must be remembered that both these acts—currency reform and initial liberalization—were passed without a proper parliament, before the creation of the Federal Republic. Erhard himself said later: "Judging from all subsequent experience, we may rightfully assert that no government and no parliament would have had the nerve, later on, to introduce and defend the system of free market economy."[6]

The negative image which most of the "de-actions" created because of their implementation by the victorious Allies was soon replaced by positive impressions. Even the "unjust" currency reform, which left untouched, to a great extent, the substance of "real" possessions such as real estate, shares, and enterprises, and which had been enforced by Allied authorities against the wish of Germans who had wanted to link the reform with a concurrent law equalizing the war and postwar burden (*Lastenausgleichsgesetz*, enacted in 1952), became past history. With long-forgotten goods and services reappearing, with money reassuming real purchasing power, and with personal incomes slowly catching up with price rises and finally surpassing them, a majority of Germans acclaimed the new market system.

It may be considered indicative of this change of public opinion that the "de-actions" were soon represented as reliberalizations. The process was regarded as one liberating the economy for free enterprise, creative competition, and unrestricted pursuit of private income by each individual. The idea that economic, business, and labor activity should be entirely nonpolitical was reintroduced into West German thinking. The feeling was reinforced that "political" interventions in the economic process were indicative of a totalitarian state, such as they had known under the Nazis or as they now witnessed next door in the Soviet Occupation Zone.

Dogmatic, principle-ridden planners had to withdraw step by step. The Social Democrats who, during the first years, had most heavily opposed Erhard's policy finally ended up with a program which only mildly deviates from the one which Erhard proclaims (and which certainly is less to the left than the CDU program that Adenauer's party started with in a very leftist climate immediately after the war).[7] The nation embraced an economic policy concept called *Soziale Marktwirtschaft*. Though this is sometimes translated as meaning something like "welfare state,"[8] it is nevertheless the description of an economic system in which the financing, investment, production, distribution, and allocation processes are to be regulated by free prices, free wages, and free competition, while government is held responsible for growth in general and for the rules of the game. Even if the concept were understood otherwise by its theoretical designers, it was this liberalist creed (not always liberalist practice) which was reintroduced into West German business after 1948.

This theoretical "system" is primarily associated with the name of Ludwig Erhard, director of bi- and tri-zonal economic administration from March, 1948, Minister of Economics from the creation of the Federal Republic in 1949 until 1963, elected Chancellor in 1963. Erhard had this system more or less ready for use when he started reliberalization in 1948. The Freiburg school of economic teaching and research, whose basic works had been written in seclusion during the Third Reich and were published either abroad or after the fall of the Reich,[9] can be held responsible for shaping part of it.

Briefly, the system is one in which control and direction of the economic process—although not the rules—are left to free enterprises. Practical techniques for this economic policy, as far as they were suggested by theorists of *Soziale Marktwirtschaft* at all, consisted of (a) liberalizing all goods and services as far as could be done with some justification, (b) setting up strict rules preventing cartel and trust-monopolizing practices, (c) guaranteeing nonintervention of state or pressure group power inconsistent with the semi-automatic process of market movements,[10] and (d) creating and maintaining a money mechanism producing stable money and steady growth. (But such a money mechanism, on which neoliberalists could not agree, remains as yet undiscovered.)[11] Measures consistent with the system had to be global and neutral. If specific, nonglobal measures had to be taken, they had either to consist of "de-actions," such as abolition of former specific interventions in the market process, or of transitional acts helping a particular section of the economy to adjust to movements already started by the market.

The main reliberalizing measures taken since 1948 are listed here in the order of their enactment:

> 1948—Four days after currency reform, removal of dozens of decrees controlling and fixing prices of consumer goods, including some foodstuffs.[12]
>
> 1948—Changes in the income tax which the Allies had raised, in 1946, to confiscatory levels.[13]
>
> 1948—Abolition of the wage freeze and restoration of free collective bargaining.[14]
>
> 1949–50—Abolition of last rationing measures in the field of food (but maintenance of artificial food prices by the government).[15]
>
> 1950—Another lowering of income tax levels.[16]
>
> 1952—Readmission of "buying on the margin" in commodity exchanges (although not in stock exchanges).
>
> 1957—Law restricting cartels and monopolies.[17]
>
> 1959—Removal of last restrictions to foreign monetary

transactions; import of goods liberalized to 91.8 per cent (from OEEC countries), 85.3 per cent (dollar countries).[18]

1959—Beginning of denationalization, re-privatization of some firms, e.g., part of Preussag capital sold to public.[19]

1960—Beginning of lifting of rent control, liberalizing housing.[20]

1960—Volkswagen capital partially sold to public.[21]

Some reliberalization measures were not effected by legislative or executive laws and decrees but by court decisions, e.g., the decision allowing free competition among pharmacies formerly organized in a sort of guild protectionist group. Another part of the liberalizing drive was carried out by international bodies such as the Coal and Steel Community or the European Economic Community. Among these were the following:

1951—Treaty on the institution of a European Coal and Steel Community (Montanunion), establishing a common market for these goods among six European countries.[22]

1957—Treaty on the institution of a European Economic Community among the same six countries, encompassing a Customs Union.[23]

In the course of the years following the currency reform and the recovery of West Germany after the Korean crisis, the economy developed most "miraculously." The phrase *Deutsches Wirtschaftswunder* ("German economic miracle") was coined. The growth figures in Table 1 suggest the magnitude of the progress.

The West Germans (whose population had increased from 38.7 million in 1937 to 50 million in 1955, partly because of an influx of 8.7 million refugees from the East) took the removal of all restrictions on private business activity as a signal for a restless and sometimes reckless drive for compensating and overcompensating for all losses and damages suffered in the war, the Nazi terror, and the Great Depression. The main drive of most Germans, workers and employers alike, became *"enrichissez-vous."*[24] The average weekly working hours of industrial workers increased from 39.8 in 1947 to 49.4 in 1956. This was not due to pressures exerted by government or business. The West Germans wanted almost total self-determination after nine years of totalitarianism. And self-determination meant (ahead of family and private life) dedication to work, business, income, and consumption. Above all, it meant the reacquisition of durable consumer goods.

The reconstruction of the productive apparatus was financed, after an initial impetus of $1.5 billion in Marshall Plan aid (from

TABLE I (Federal Territory)

	1938	1952	1961
Gross National Product (in bill. DM/RM actual prices)	47.8	126	310.4
Production:			
electric energy (mill. kwh)	31,096	56,208	124,563
oil (1000 tons)	552	1,755	6,776
iron from ore (1000 tons)	3,072	4,097	5,011
coal (1000 tons)	138,501	125,064	142,741
cement (1000 tons)	15,262 (Reich)	12,886	28,593
steel (1000 tons)	17,902	15,806	33,458
automobiles	205,137	317,684	1,903,975
trucks	55,735	110,151	243,323
All industrial production (1950 = 100)	107.3	125.9	262
Index of living costs (1938 = 100)	100	171.5	192.6

Source: *Statistiches Jahrbuch der Bundesrepublik Deutschland.*

April, 1948, to December, 1954),[25] by the classical financing instruments of underdeveloped peoples—government investments and self-financing by individual firms.[26] As a result, the newly formed fortunes were distributed in quite a one-sided manner. Combined with the one-sidedness of the currency reform, this produced unrest, especially among the have-nots. Although this unrest was voiced politically by Social Democrats, for instance, and by labor unions, it had no major social effect. Moreover, two currency reforms within twenty-five years obviously have changed the concept of wealth. The ideal of the middle class is no longer the *rentier* who lives on the interest earned by a private fortune. Rather, the man who can expect a reasonable social security pension is considered "rich" and—most significantly—much more secure than an owner of private capital.

Stock speculation remained by no means unknown and even increased with the growth of private funds, the re-creation of the capital market, and the introduction of small shares and investment funds. The government itself created a new wave of popular speculation when it issued, on the occasion of the privatization of the Volkswagen plant, small shares which were sold with a special "social rebate" to low income earners. But this sort of "people's capitalism" merely meant a special means of hoarding cash until it could or would be spent for acquisition of consumer goods, automobiles or, at best, small houses. It was neither a participation in the stock of the economy's productive capital nor a form of family savings for old age security.[27]

Whereas in West Germany production and income rose to peaks unknown before the war, the Soviet Occupation Zone, which was split from the body of the Reich with the currency reform in 1948 and later turned into a separate political unit (Deutsche Demokratische Republik, DDR), showed no marked success in its economic activity. Production figures are difficult to compare, not only because of the veil usually cast over these reports in countries in the Soviet bloc, but also because a considerable change of economic structure—and, therefore, of the "output mix"—has been effected to counterbalance the absence of the industrialized West. At any rate, what is clear is that the consumption level in the Soviet Zone is far below that of the Federal Republic. This is, after all, what counts in the people's judgment and serves to condemn the economic system as well as the political regime of East Germany.

The general impression of the majority of the West Germans was that, granted the working spirit with which the people were imbued after the currency reform, granted Marshall aid, granted the absence and/or low rate of armament and occupation costs, granted even the reasonable behavior of organized labor and organized business alike—the bulk of responsibility for the "German economic miracle" still had to be attributed to the economic system developed after 1948. *Soziale Marktwirtschaft* meant free enterprise moderated by some global target manipulation and by some income rectification measures carried out by taxes and subsidies. It thus contrasted favorably with both the National Socialist Corporative Economy and the Communist-planned society as known in Soviet Russia since 1917, experienced again next door in the Soviet Occupation Zone since 1945. A majority of the people identified the system with "success." They not only voted for it in four federal and various Länder elections,[28] they also believed it would function at other times and places. In other words, "controlled free enterprise" is not only credited with being a workable machine for the special situation of German reconstruction after total war damage in mid-twentieth century, it is considered a prescription and remedy for any kind of situation. Hence, "Erhard's system" becomes a creed one must adhere to. It occupies the place of former and rival ideologies. Most significantly, its economic policy is linked with parliamentarian democracy as the political prerequisite for good behavior in the Western community.[29]

Any kind of planning, centralized or decentralized, which approaches economic processes via macroeconomic channels and treats microeconomic units with macroeconomic tools is viewed askance not only as ineffective economically and "less rational" but as politically dangerous and superfluous. *Planification à la française,* the Monnet program, and the office of the *Commissariat au Plan,* knowledge of which has been spreading in Germany because of French pressure for adoption of their system within the Common Market, is viewed skeptically.[30] The West Germans say in effect: "You have reconstructed your economy after the war with a series of five-year plans, executed with the help of a nationalized credit system, and you have produced in ten years a rate of industrial growth of 111 per cent and a rate of inflation of 162 per cent. We in West Germany have, starting from a much more devastated base, achieved our reconstruction without explicit planning but with the help of free competition and a private or denationalized credit system, and we produced a growth rate of 163 per cent in the same ten years, with a 39 per cent rate of inflation."

GOVERNMENT INTERVENTION

The neoliberal creed has so far not succeeded in making quite clear which techniques of government or group intervention are considered to be consistent with the market, neutral to the system (*"marktkonform"*), or inimical to the market.[31] There is a prominent, complicated struggle over whether a particular government intervention can be considered as neutral, hence legitimate, or not. And there is a list of government interventions which even those neoliberalists who helped to effect them will admit are inconsistent with their system.

These measures, then, have to be justified in other ways. What is their place, what is their meaning within government policy, and what is their function with respect to the spectacular growth process of the West German economy? Have they hampered, supported, or even, as some heretics argue, have they, and not the liberal measures, produced this growth? In order to answer, it is necessary to describe the scope and nature of the interventionist measures put forth by German central and Länder governments since 1948. The following series of economic policy actions were meant to influence the economic process in a way the market would not itself have automatically chosen.

Monetary Techniques

Influencing the economic process by influencing the money flow is a classical device of archliberalist economic policy as well as modern fiscal policy. Many scientific supporters of Erhard and his group consider such monetary interventions to be definitely consistent with a market system.[32] The underlying idea may be that in this case monetary policy has a universalizing effect which the law would otherwise have to achieve in other ways.[33] The levying of taxes and/or distribution of subsidies does not force (by decrees, orders, or even violence) anyone to do or to neglect certain things. One merely receives increases or cuts in income, and this works as a "signal" rather than as an order. Above all, monetary policy is regarded as rendering government action anonymous.

The question is whether the following measures, purely monetary, can still be considered anonymous in this sense:

(1) 1951 Investment Aid Act.[34] Provided for a compulsory loan of one billion marks to cover initial investment needs of coal mining, iron- and steel-producing industries, and energy (including water power), and lorry production of Federal Railways. Every business existing in January, 1951, was forced to contribute to the raising of the sum and was given (or, if possible, could choose among) securities issued by receiving industries. The collector and distributor was a special bank (*Industriekreditbank*). The act has been much de-

bated. There have been law suits up to the highest federal courts to test its constitutionality.[35]

(2) 1949 Refugee Aid Measures and 1953 Federal Expellee Act. Special tax and credit privileges; agreement among Länder on resettling expellees in order to help out Länder with highest refugee quotas.[36]

(3) 1949 measures to equalize war burdens and 1952 *Lastenausgleichsgesetz*.[37] An attempt to distribute as equally as possible, ex post facto, all economic costs of the war, the Allied Occupation, and the currency reform, including air raids and loss of private property owing to loss of territory. To this should be added the *Bundesentschädigungsgesetze* of 1953 and 1956,[38] which regulated restitution to victims of injustice suffered under the Third Reich. Technically, the *Lastenausgleich* constitutes a special tax system, with a special treasury from which subsidies, indemnities, and restitution of various sorts are paid.

(4) Housing Construction Aid. First law in 1950, second in 1956,[39] measures for income tax exemptions on housing construction, and the Act on Allocation of Housing in 1953.[40] The whole system was designed to increase housing construction so as to replace the 22 per cent of all dwelling space lost in the war (not counting houses in lost territories). The scope of this aid can be seen from these few statistics:[41]

	1939	1945	1955	1961
Number of dwelling units (*Wohnungen*) in millions	10.3	8.1	12.1	15.8

Financing of housing construction, in percentages of GNP, amounted to 2.6 on the average between 1925 and 1938, 6.1 in 1955. From 1952 on, about one-half million dwelling units have been constructed annually, compared with less than 200,000 in prewar times. The two construction aid acts were planned to subsidize 1.8 million dwelling units each, which amounts to nearly 50 per cent of all houses being built with government aid. To this has to be added house construction subsidized indirectly by tax exemptions. Until 1955 all construction costs (for houses built for personal use or for others, such as employees) were income tax exempt; since then 25 per cent of costs are tax exempt.

(5) Other investment, construction, and similar aid based on tax exemption, tax reduction, or depreciation allowances. Instead of lowering the entire income tax level, as Erhard asked, Allied authorities agreed in 1949 to "specified measures," lowering taxes on particular activities. The result was a "Swiss cheese" income tax law.[42] It is difficult to appraise the effect of these measures since they are so particularized. It has also proved difficult to repeal some of them, since the people concerned have become so accustomed to them. Examples are tax exemption originally intended to encourage ship construction to help build a merchant service and exemption of taxes on earnings which are not withdrawn but reinvested in businesses not subject to corporation tax.

(6) Family Allowance Act of 1954.[43] In addition to general tax deductions according to the number of children in a family, special children's allowances were introduced giving cash money to parents for the third (later revised to the second) and additional children.

(7) Various laws designed to increase saving by giving special premium allowances, or tax exemption for savings, or special provisions for savings which are reinvested in the employer's firm. In this way, a portion of the wages is turned into a sort of "investment wage" (*Investivlohn*).[44]

(8) Subsidies to coal mining given in an indirect way by subsidizing housing construction for miners, or by forcing accident insurance associations of other industries to support the insurance associations of the mining industry.[45]

(9) Punitive taxes. For example, special real estate taxes are levied to punish landowners who do not construct houses on their property.[46]

(10) Discriminatory actions taken by the Central Bank against foreign money either by prohibiting payment of interest, by forbidding the opening of certain types of bank accounts, by preventing foreign investment in German bonds, or levying a special tax rate on such investment. These measures were meant to defend German currency against "hot

money" and were especially applied in the period before the reevaluation of the Deutsche Mark in 1961, and in 1963.[47]

(11) In 1959 the Minister of Finance replied to a public question in the federal parliament on the extent of federal subsidies, including tax exemptions and reductions.[48] Of direct subsidies, the government paper listed sixty-five single measures recorded in the 1959 federal budget (federal only), amounting to 2.7 billion marks. Indirect subsidies (by tax exemption, etc.) were provided in 149 special laws, legal provisions, decrees, or parts of other laws which, all in all, amounted to a diminution of 4 billion marks in tax income— as far as it could be estimated. Social security subsidies were not included.

Nonmonetary Techniques

Nonmonetary intervention techniques serve mainly to constrain market functioning, for example by fixing or controlling prices or levels of output, or by influencing over-all economic structure. They have to be analyzed with great precision down to their remote effects in order to determine the extent of their effect on a system allegedly organized as a market economy. There are, among others, the following:

(1) Market regulations (*Marktordnungen*) relating to the agricultural sector and its products, including sugar, grain, butter, and meat. In 1955, regulating offices (*Einfuhrund Vorratsstellen*) were created to maintain government-fixed prices by buying and selling, regulating imports and exports. The alleged aim of this protective legislation is to rationalize the agricultural structure and elevate the level of knowledge of the agrarian population.[49]

(2) Special regulation of the banking and insurance sector, dating back to the 1930's.[50] Government boards have control functions over private banking and insurance (apart from the authority of the Central Bank, which has another basis). Private banking is exempt from the Anticartel Act. Some cooperative actions of banks are under government supervision and endorsed by it, e.g., a cartel on interest paid by banks to

holders of accounts (*Habenzins-Abkommen*). Interest paid by debtors to banks is government regulated.

(3) Codetermination Act of 1951, applying to basic industries.[51] This law continued a measure originally instituted by Allied authorities to help control the Ruhr industrialists. Labor is given 50 per cent of the votes in the supervisory councils of shareholding companies in basic industries (coal and steel) and in addition furnishes a member of the top management board whose task is personnel direction (*Arbeitsdirektor*). Labor delegates are elected by shopworkers from candidate, some of whom may be outsiders, presented by unions—a definitely noncapitalist measure giving nonowners decisive influence on industrial plants. The result cannot yet be judged.[52] Labor has so far suffered from a shortage of able men to be delegated to the boards. What is clear is that labor has not used the opportunity to integrate the business policies of various firms.

(4) The law regulating "constitution of enterprises," passed one year later (1952),[53] was much more liberal in outlook, in delineating the rights and duties of workers' councils and shop stewards. However, it also prescribed that the boards of all corporations not covered by the Codetermination Act should have at least one-third workers' representatives.

(5) Exemption of specific groups and of particular practices from the Anticartel Act, such as organized labor and management, banking, insurance, railroads, and price fixing by producers.

(6) Shop Closing Act, establishing compulsory closing hours for all stores and shops.[54]

(7) Laws or legal clauses providing aid for special zones, such as frontier zones and regions with emergencies, within the federal territory.[55] The Ministry for Housing Construction was renamed the Ministry for Housing, Town Construction and Spatial Order.

(8) Social Security Revision-Act, of 1957.[56] The need for a reorganization of all government insurance had become imperative after years of war, destruction, inflation, and currency reform. The reorganization could have been regarded

simply as a sort of "reliberalization" measure were it not for the fact that it created three instruments of an almost revolutionary character:

a. Extension of compulsory government insurance to all employees with a monthly income below 1,250 marks (formerly 800 marks, currently 1,800 marks);

b. Suspension of ordinary insurance business principles for capital coverage of future charges, replaced with a turnover system;

c. Introduction of compulsory linkage of all social security pensions to a formula of mixed wage and productivity indices (*"Dynamisierung"*). Newly granted pensions were automatically linked to the indices. Existing pensions had to be linked by vote, on the recommendation of a specially formed "Council of Experts" (*Sozialbeirat*).

(9) Construction Curtailment Act of 1962.[57] Sharply restricts both public and private construction activity by strictly prohibiting certain types of construction. The act was designed to curb a marked price rise in the construction business which was mainly attributed to excessive government activity in this field.

(10) In this context, a court decision which illustrates the situation in a special section of the economy must be mentioned. An act of 1927 had created the Federal Unemployment Insurance and Registry Office as a state employment service monopoly. After World War II several private agents took up the business of providing top personnel to firms, and one such agent was subjected to a law suit by the government. The agent was held to have violated the law of 1927, although there is common agreement that the central registry office for top personnel which the federal government has set up in Frankfurt has not proved effective, and all corporations are dependent upon the private agents.

Finally, there are continuing government examinations in an attempt to make the country's economic structure clearer. A government inquiry[58] into the extent of business concentration (published in 1964) held that the degree of concentration, especially when judged in the light of coming increases in international markets, was not alarming. Another inquiry was requested by Chancellor Erhard in his 1963 inauguration speech, an inquiry into the state of reallocation measures for "social" purposes.[59] It is presumed that many individuals paying taxes are being subsidized by these same taxes. Reallocation legislation has developed into a jungle of interrelations which no one can penetrate. There is a demand for a "table of social transfers" to clear away this jungle and show who benefits and who loses from all these reallocations.

Those officially responsible for shaping neoliberalist economic policy must justify the acts of intervention enumerated above, and they try to do so. In the long run, they say, government will regularly limit itself to two types of action: (1) establishing, enforcing, and guaranteeing the rules of the market game, including free competition and neutral money, and (2) regulating the whole economic process to produce stability of money, of exchange rates, of growth, and full employment. In the short run, intervention might be necessary to help certain branches of the economy adjust to structural changes created or revealed by the technological process and market movements.[60] Most of the nonmonetary measures are designed to be such "adjustment measures," serving—instead of opposing—the market process. One of the best illustrations of this point of view is the set of agricultural market regulations which are all meant to adjust West German agriculture to modern technological methods and requirements. If money payments are made, they are earmarked for investment purposes and not for the purpose of increasing the personal income of individual farmers.

Let us set aside for the moment the fact that the farmers' organizations and their pressure groups have different aims. (They demand income for the farmer on a par with the industrial worker's or businessman's income.) Let us take the adjustment argument at face value. Then the "adjusting" measures designed by legislation or by administrative regulation produce an effect which is difficult for a neoliberal economy to digest. This situation is aggravated by the number and inconsistency of the measures.

The West German federal parliament alone passed 1,726 laws from its first session in the fall of 1949 to the session opening the summer vacation period in 1964.[61] Most of these concerned economic financial, or social policy. This does not include the innumerable laws of the Länder (state) parliaments and municipal and county diets and the thousands of decrees, "explanatory regulations," and the like, issued by all sorts of executive branch administrations.

Engaging in any business activity, and even working in the labor force, requires, apart from the appropriate skills, additional training for complying with the various government regulations to which one is subject. This is no longer "free enterprise" pure and simple; there is too much administration involved in the market.

How the allegedly free-operating individual is controlled becomes much more obvious when one passes from the number of interventions to their financial importance. Through income taxes the state participates by more than one-half (of the peak incomes) in the results of economic activity. In West Germany almost 40 per cent of the GNP is channeled through and controlled by fiscal, parafiscal, and other public budgets, not including government participation in private business, joint stockholding companies, and cooperative enterprises.

The vast extent of public control of the economy raises many problems of consistency among government policies. There have been many instances in the Federal Republic of a lamentable lack of coordination—as it is usually called. This applies to coordination between governmental levels, such as federal and Länder, to coordination within one governmental level, and even to coordination of legislative or administrative measures emanating from a single source. In 1965, for example, as already mentioned, the federal parliament passed a law to curtail building activity in order to control the construction boom and its high prices.[62] The law went so far as to prohibit, in certain situations, construction of houses for governmental and private agents. It was passed at a time when an earlier law that had been designed to promote construction in municipal areas was still in effect.[63] With the two laws effective, a proprietor could be, at the same time, forbidden to build and punished for not doing it. A law suit has been brought before the Supreme Constitutional Court to eliminate this contradiction.

Instances of inconsistency of government action in which a subordinate measure conflicts with the proclaimed, over-all economic targets (such as full employment, price stability, exchange rate stability, and harmonious growth) are also frequent. Some government interventions even conflict directly with basic principles of a market economy, such as free prices. In 1962, Erhard, then Minister of Economics, countered a price rise of Volkswagen by psychological retaliation, and finally by a lowering of tariffs laid on foreign competitors' automobile models.[64]

The most serious examples indicate how little coordination there is between federal ministries. One cause is the proliferation of agencies involved. There were, in June, 1964, fifteen ministries (out of twenty-one) directly concerned with economic questions—economics, finance, labor, food and agriculture, refugees, economic cooperation with underdeveloped countries, foreign affairs, research, housing, etc. (In 1914, there were seven comparable ministries [Reichsämter], of which three had economic tasks.)[65] Today the other fiscal agents—such as social security treasuries or the Central Bank, which by law has the status of a ministry—are included.

The lack of integration begins with index figures on economic development and price movements which differ—sometimes substantially—even on past events, and it ends with quarrels which sometimes prevent action. Most notable has been the fight for control of economic foreign policy: a board of emissaries from all the ministries involved has been set up, but the board usually proves ineffective against the dominance of the Ministry of Foreign Affairs.[66] In some cases, however, the Minister of Finance or the Minister of Agriculture prevails. In this situation, standing orders of the cabinet can become more important than articles of the Constitution.

These fights for control indicate that particular ministries (not to say their ministers) exhibit a narrow attitude toward official economic philosophy. Thus, the Ministry of Economics has been labeled the "Ministry for Market Principles and Middle Class Promises," whereas the Ministry of Finance has been the Agency for the Protection or Fostering of Larger Industrial Units.[67]

The Ministry of Food and Agriculture (official name: Ministerium für Ernährung, Landwirtschaft und Forsten) is sometimes sarcastically called "Ministry for the Feeding of Agriculture."

The problems created by the extent and the internal inconsistency of governmental economic activity have led to a demand heard quite often. If, it is pointed out, "the state" is already controlling so many money transactions and so much economic activity, it should at least coordinate its expenditures by planning or programing—but leave "the private sector" outside the reach of the programing. This is usually accompanied by the demand to extend the annual budgetary periods to several years, preferably four- to five-year plans, such as are used in private business and are considered necessary for government budgets.[68]

The following arguments usually silence these demands, however: first, there is no one state budget but thousands of federal, Länder, and local budgets whose coexistence guarantees some sort of Law of Great Number, if not competition, among fiscal agents, and whose condensation into one centralized agency controlling 40 per cent of the GNP would make it entirely unfeasible to maintain private competition within the "private sector" of the remaining 60 per cent.

Secondly, the public budgets, though about 80 per cent of their figures are generally "frozen," are still the results of competition, conflict, and compromise between various groups in parliaments and diets, and it pays to maintain them in such a bargaining situation in order to assure the freedom of the remaining 60 per cent of the "private sector."

Finally, to preserve the play of the market forces within the private realm, one must in principle abstain from any attempt to plan the actions of the government sector as long as government interventions in the economy are subject to market forces. Public budgets are *money* "plans." Government is as much concerned with the cyclic movements of prices and the free interplay of its partners (including collective bargaining of state officials and their unions) as any other contractor in the economy.

The Future: Problems and Plans

The weighty problems facing the West German economy require thorough investigation and concerted action. Some of them are so urgent and so difficult as to push the controversy described above to a showdown. Before attempting to disentangle conflicting views, it may help to outline briefly the challenge now encountered by West Germany that necessitates reflection on policy principles and tools.

At least since the Great Depression of 1929–33, even the most devoted advocates of free market principles do not deny the need for some agency to do something to secure a reasonable measure of full employment and some attenuation of grave business cycles. It has become generally—though sometimes grudgingly—accepted that the government (at least the Central Bank) is in some way responsible for economic development without major crises or, the specialist's language, for "harmonious growth." Some people even argue that guaranteeing economic well-being has become the first principle of legitimacy in modern democracies.[69]

However, there is much debate on what all this implies in practice. In West Germany, it begins with the controversy over how much microeconomic data should be collected for macroeconomic use: should there be macroeconomic national accounting? If so, of what sort: universal or sectoral, ex post facto statements only, or prognostic figures also, indicative forecasts only, or programing with some sort of compulsory power? Here, a wide variety of opinions have been aired,[70] but actions taken so far have been very cautious. The last significant action was the passing of a law in 1963, establishing an expert advisory council of five people to submit opinions on macroeconomic development, after much debate on how far the experts' authority should go.[71]

Some of the pressing matters which may influence discussion— and perhaps even decision—on the role of macroeconomic analysis and tools are, as of 1964:

(1) *Planification à la française,* which enters the discussion on German economic policy via the Brussels agencies of the European Economic Community. There is no doubt that the high commissioners, even President Hallstein, have ideas somewhat different from the official German view of what ought to be done. Indeed, an open debate has taken place between Erhard and Hallstein in the Strasbourg parliamentary council.[72]

(2) The constant danger of "importing inflation" and other domestic threats to the currency. These demand thoughtful care and ready action, and some economists and even observers in some foreign countries consider such watchfulness the price of prosperity. However, a stable money policy, which would have been impossible within the gold currency system, represents, when viewed systematically, a form of "planned"

economic policy, even if the chief executor is not the government but the Central Bank. Erhard has never missed any occasion to state his stout resolution to protect the currency as the chief vehicle of sound market principles.[73] There are some who interpret Article 20, Section 1, of the West German Basic Law as a constitutional demand to legislate and govern for stable money. Discretionary measures taken against foreign money-holders in order to fight imported inflation have already intimated that "stable money" is, when incorporated into the administrative legal system, not a "general law" consistent with market principles which allow for free movement of all economic agents and goods, but a government program. The same holds true, of course, for "full employment" and "harmonious growth."

The implications of the allegedly dominant stable money policy of the West German government became clear with the official action taken to counter the price rise announced by a business firm, Volkswagen, mentioned above.[74] The action was meant to influence business psychology more than actual cash flow, and in the end Volkswagen maintained its price increase.

(3) Growing armament expenditures (including international military transactions), growing international cooperation in economic aid to underdeveloped countries, and international joint economic actions of other sorts. These demand comprehensive exploration and—even if only to enable serious debate of alternatives—macroeconomic analysis.

(4) Urgent need for fiscal reform to reallocate tax revenue and budget charges between federal, Länder, and local level requires deliberation on macroeconomic principles. The "fiscal constitution" of West Germany is still dominated by political federalist thinking.[75]

(5) The growing affluent society at home. Widespread evidence of this growth emphasizes the dependence of economic growth processes on increases in private demand. On the other hand, many public utilities and facilities are lagging behind private consumption—even more so than in other countries. Roads, railroads, schools, universities, scientific research, and underdeveloped regions in the country require (if only for

economy in taxes and budgetary expenditures) organized action, based on macroeconomic analysis.

(6) All this is aggravated by a growing need for an organized income policy on the part of all political—not only governmental—agents. This should include not only collective bargaining agreements which are now entirely free of legal intervention in Germany, but also all kinds of "social policy." As mentioned above, social security (and now accident) pensions are linked by law to real wage levels. Some subsidizing grants—such as the "Green Plan" regulating farm subsidies—have also practically acquired an indexed status.

(7) The continuing improvement of economic science increases the possibility of political application of macroeconomic thinking. In both macro- and microeconomics, mathematics has introduced additional precision in areas where heretofore superficial guessing had ruled (game theory, operations research, linear programing, etc.). But those responsible for shaping policy have not yet gone very far in investigating the applicability of all this to economic policy in West Germany.

(8) Special cyclical situations almost invariably reveal that the instruments which governmental agencies or the Central Bank are expected to apply and/or control are not sufficient.[76] With the exception of growing unemployment and the drop in money resources for a short time in 1950 before the Korean crisis boom, no very critical situation has yet developed. So far the authorities have been very lucky, but the situation is subject to change.

Private individuals, groups and firms, and government agencies themselves are quick to affirm that they trust the chest of public anticyclical tools kept ready in case the "self-healing tendencies" of *Soziale Marktwirtschaft* should gravely fail. They say, too, that they are certain that these instruments will be "consistent" with market principles.

One cannot accurately fortell the difficulties or indicate the planning needs that would ensue should any of the above possibilities come to a head. Since 1929, when the Great Depression perplexed politicians and economists alike, Germans have learned a great deal about the seemingly irrational forces of the market, of competition and speculation. Whether this understanding (which is not necessarily identical with businessmen's experience) can be applied to a market economy while maintaining its essential character has not yet been put to a test in West Germany.

The "Social Market" Model

Arguments about theories of economic systems carried on in the Federal Republic of Germany since 1948 are never merely theoretical debates or scientific disputes. They are of the utmost practical importance for two reasons. First, if they express the pragmatic experience and knowledge of expert technicians on the machinery of macroeconomics, everybody interested in the functioning of this machinery welcomes the debate as a practical means of sharpening the instruments of social science. Second, an argument on economic systems might reveal allegiance or at least adherence to political groups, and then the practical benefit may be a clarification of political issues.

To appreciate both the technical and political reasons, it is necessary to understand the economic system theories as they have been described and debated in West Germany. It is one of these which now serves as a model—and provides the formula—for economic policy. The phraseology which has developed in this field derives mostly from the neoliberalist school of economics of the late Walter Eucken, although this school holds a concept of *"Soziale Marktwirtschaft"* slightly different from that held by politicians.

NEOLIBERALISM AND "SOZIALE MARKTWIRTSCHAFT"

Eucken divides the period of the industrial revolution into two epochs: the long epoch of "laissez faire policy" up to World War I and the shorter one of the "economic policy of experiments."[1]

The first, the policy of Manchester liberalism, is described as leaving the formulation of the rules, the framework and the eco-

33

nomic process therein, and the daily fight for quantity and price up to the individual economic agents. The results have been grave disturbances of the market and of monetary equilibrium by the development of monopolistic or oligopolistic markets, countervailing powers, and arbitrary monetary systems. These results and the two world wars paved the way for the stage of experimentalism in economic policy which developed two forms of organization: the "centrally administered economy" (*Zentralverwaltungswirtschaft*) and the "economic policy of the middle road."

Central economic administration can best be studied in the Soviet Union after 1928, Eucken said in 1948, though, as a model, central administration is also possible in a society which maintains the institution of private property (as did National Socialism until the end).[2] The positive result of such a central order is, according to neoliberalists, its technical efficiency, but this is counterbalanced by negative social results. Political and civil freedom, rule of law, or preservation of spontaneity cannot be guaranteed by a centrally administered economic system, with or without collective property. Collective property, moreover, cannot be maintained side by side with a competitive economy; it leads to the central control of investment.

In the second experimental system, the middle road, we find a combination of the full employment policy of Keynes and Beveridge, partial centralization of the economic process, such as nationalization of basic industries, and a new form of the corporate state. All three, prevalent in the non-Fascist West from 1929–33 until today, are criticized by the neoliberalists because, at best, they regulate the economic process but not the "economic order" (market forms, monetary system, etc.). They do not eliminate periods of disequilibrium. Therefore, they, too, finally end up with central economic administration as the systematic solution. What condemns the experimental systems is just the fact that they have nothing to offer but their experimentalism.[3]

In contrast, the neoliberalist's system, which claims to avoid the pitfalls of laissez faire as well as of central administration and moderate experimentalism, is based on principles rather than on pragmatic experiment. These principles are: (1) The creation or restoration of a functioning price system based on full and true competition, which has to be made the touchstone of each economic policy measure, and (2) All attempts to achieve a competitive order are in vain so long as a certain monetary stability is not secured.[4]

The two principles—safeguard the market and safeguard the money—are being made constitutional principles of the West German economy. This, and not their existence, is new. But the question remains whether safeguarding is actually possible and how it can be made practicable. The chief designer of neoliberalism, Walter Eucken, died before his principles could be put to the critical test. His book on economic policy was edited only after his death. As for monetary policy, the editor probably was doubtful about some of Eucken's practical proposals for monetary reform (which went in the direction of Graham's commodity currency much debated on both sides of the ocean). In the popular issue of Eucken's book these are suppressed.[5]

The problem of how a present-day monetary system could be consistent with market principles is still in the "if" and "how" stage. Money should, says Eucken, function as "automatically" as possible, just as the competitive system does in general.[6] Here Eucken's neoliberalism is corrected by Müller-Armack, the theoretical designer of Erhard's policy and the first practical executor of the design as secretary of state in Erhard's government. Müller-Armack gave the term *Soziale Markwirtschaft* its special, ambivalent meaning as both a "social" market economy (meaning "just," with regard to the people) and a "regulated" market economy (meaning "controlled").[7]

As to the problem of social justice, Eucken himself thought that "a policy restoring complete competition does not suffice to insure justice in all problems of social life," and he called for a social policy designed by the government—in addition to his "principles."[8]

Much more important is the problem of *"gesteuerte Marktwirtschaft,"* the regulation of the market in its entirety. Müller-Armack describes a modern market economy as half automatic but leaning toward manipulation and regulation as a whole. It is the monetary system which is usually applied as the regulating mechanism of the whole. But if it is to be the main regulator, it cannot be left "automatic" as desired by Eucken. In fact, if the appropriate monetary system has not been found and enforced (and it has not), there are still lacking both principles and mechanisms to key problems in the areas of growth, cyclical policy, full employment, foreign exchange, and the price level.

In other words, neither neoliberalism nor *Soziale Marktwirtschaft* offers viable systems or techniques to master, by themselves, the most important global problems of a modern economy. What they offer are vague "principles" (*Grundsätze*), and even they are shaky. Thus Eucken closed his book on economic policy with two principles for state action: (1) Governmental policy should aim at dissolving economic power groups or at least limiting their sphere of operation, and (2) Political-economic activity of government should aim at the establishment of economic order, not at the regulation (*Lenkung*) of the economic process.[9]

Neoliberalism does not, in principle, exclude state intervention in the market. It merely aims at rigorously excluding measures which might disturb the market system or threaten to destroy free price and wage formation. Intervention is allowed if it leaves intact the money (price) mechanism even if it produces a change in equilibrium resulting in a price other than might have been formed "automatically" without such intervention. Here is a justification for all sorts of reallocative transfer methods carried out by government budgets or parafiscal agents, a procedure that has, in West Germany as elsewhere, been used to a very great extent.

There is a tendency among practical businessmen and journalists to oppose such transfers simply because of their size, e.g., to warn against passing the 40 per cent limit in state participation or the 50 per cent limit in income taxes. Representatives of neoliberalist scientific research do not support this view. "Far-reaching interventions into income distribution are possible," says von Stackelberg, "without abolishing the system as such." Miksch says: "Even if the number of regulative measures that have been proved necessary to correct income distribution should be so large that in that respect there would remain no quantitative difference from the fundamental claims of advocates of a planned society, the principle (of a market society ruled by perfect competition) would not lose anything of its value."[10]

In other words, if 100 per cent of individual personal income were confiscated by taxes and redistributed by fiscal measures, a market economy would prevail if only prices and original incomes were left free to be formed by competition. Parliament, as the arena where the forces competing for redistribution would contend, would be transformed into a market or meeting place for collective bargaining between countervailing powers. It is difficult to understand, however, how the parliament could respond directly to competitive pressures and, at the same time, legislate as a neutral force for the maintenance of the competitive and monetary rules, as required by neoliberalism.

NEOLIBERALISM IN PRACTICE

The other distinguishing feature of the neoliberalist creed is the defense of pure competition and the fight against concentrated economic power, usually held responsible for "disequilibrium." Here, as in the case of control of the monetary system, the core of the problem is political rather than economic. Namely, if a technically useful instrument (for securing full employment and stable money or for fighting cartels and big business) could be found, who is going to press for its enactment against powerful, voter-backed interests?

Eucken once said: "A well-functioning competitive system will not only safeguard mankind against economic distress. It will also serve as the sole protection against the dangers of totalitarianism."[11]

In 1957, after many years of behind-the-scenes and open fights, the "law against restricting competition" (Anticartel Act) was passed.[12] It was meant by Erhard to be a strictly prohibitive law, with exceptions only after due process. It came out, after much bickering, with so many exceptions that the prohibitive essence could be declared dead. Moreover, although it may be possible to enforce a ban against cartels which can come into being only with the consent of several individuals, big business itself cannot be outlawed so simply. As a consequence, small business complains that it is strictly forbidden to organize in cartels, which are in many cases their only means of resisting big business.[13]

Market deformations by power and agreement are no more and no less frequent in West Germany under the alleged rule of competition than elsewhere in comparable non-Communist societies. If there are no strictly "administered prices" (because there are no monopolies or cartel agreements in the strict sense), at least there is disequilibrium caused by countervailing forces. The assertion that the only just and feasible remedy should be the crushing of economic power is, even in West Germany, often attacked as not only impractical from the side of economic efficiency, but also incompatible with social realism.[14] The bulk of the population does not demand economic reconversion to *"petit bourgeois* principles," but rather adaptation to an age of nuclear technology and cybernetics.[15]

Critics—not all of whom deserve the reproach of having been born in a socialist cradle—intimate that, after all, there is no substantial difference between laissez faire liberalism and neoliberalism in principle. Their essential features are very similar: private property (and from it the derived autonomy of investment); liberty of contracts, including wages, prices and interest; private production for private consumption; and public demand allowed only as much as provided for by public consent to taxes and budgets given *ad hoc* in parliaments elected freely from among private and autonomous economic agents. Neoliberalism, according to these critics, is simply nineteenth-century liberalism minus gold currency plus government responsibility for global targets of economic development (a necessary consequence of abolition of gold as the currency regulator) plus a larger percentage of reallocating transfer payments.

Other scholars and observers, of a more moderate political bent, might be tempted to add that the broadening of the areas of government intervention and government ownership of enterprises has meantime transformed the system into a "mixed economy." This is here understood to mean a mixture of market principles as practiced before 1914 and central administration as practiced during the prewar phase of the Third Reich or even as in Soviet Russia. Especially when proclaimed by "practical men," "mixed economy" is often used to close any debate on policy as well as on systems, ideologies, and dogmas.[16]

Obviously, the problem of systematic economic analysis (indispensable for rational economic action by both business and government) is not solved by coining new labels or stretching old ones.

There is very little left in West Germany of the original foe of capitalism or laissez faire liberalism: the central administration of either socialism or communism. The Communist party had already been reduced to an unimportant faction by the time it was outlawed in 1956.[17] The Social Democrats, as well as the majority of the labor unions, have almost completed the process of disavowing the Marxist creed and, therefore, the Marxist system. As far as the domestic scene is concerned, the West German economy does not see itself as actively fighting Socialist nationalization and expropriation. This opponent no longer exists at home.

This fading away of the ancient foe is confirmed by new relations which emerge between old opponents. Management and labor are more and more portrayed as competitors who are both solidly anchored in a market economy. In this respect, union leftists have moved somewhat to the right. Unions and management are also exhorted to behave as "partners," sharing common responsibility for the whole of the economy without having to be "called to reason" by state intervention. In this respect, the entrepreneurs have moved a little to the left. There still may be a great deal of estrangement between capital, management, and labor, but there is certainly no spirit of class war.

Sociologists have begun to describe the society emerging in West Germany as a "classless mass society," "prosperity society," and "welfare state."[18] The common denominator of all these labels is the notable absence of any *essential* conflict within society. There is much talk of the change or even the submergence of the "concept of opposition."[19] Socialists and Christian Democrats, businessmen and workers, farmers and retailers—all are spoken of as partners or competitors, as participants in the circular economic process, as members of a pluralistic society—but not as political friends or foes.

Yet the public forum is not without tension and discontent, even if restricted to domestic issues. There are basic antagonisms touching upon essential questions of the social order. But they are no longer expressed through actions which previously reflected political enmity, such as a strike, especially a political strike. They are carried on among "experts."[20]

The explanation seems to be that, on the one hand, expert knowledge of economic systems, on the role of mathematics in economics, on the systematic place of planning, programing, and forecasting (both coercive and informative), etc., has progressed on a worldwide scale. Macroeconomic experts are discussing hypotheses and effective solutions across national—and even East-West—borders. But, on the other hand, political and interest groups do not yet fully realize this. The results and the meaning of this technical progress have not been thoroughly digested, for instance, by the opponents of collective bargaining.

The macroeconomic experts themselves are not too happy about this. Knowing intimately the mechanism of an industrialized economy, but not necessarily attached to any one interest group, they see themselves in danger of being labeled a foe by any and all interest groups. Consequently, they tend to develop a distinct political conscience, set apart from all existing interests, claiming to serve "the interest of the whole," and yet not being able to form a cohesive group which might possibly exert political influence.

They thus find themselves in the same situation as the overwhelming majority of technologists, technicians, engineers, and natural scientists who, whether working in industry, government, or a liberal profession, may have organized themselves either in a professional-scientific association (such as a special university discipline) or as a pressure group exerting some slight influence on the market or the government in order to improve their income situation. But what they have not been able to do is to have their special, technically trained point of view used in political action—at least not in West Germany.

However, a tendency in this direction cannot be overlooked. It sometimes manifests itself in the special role of the bureaucratic expert in the government, which we shall describe later. Also the attacks on "technocrats" and "bureaucrats" which have nearly replaced the attacks against socialists are increasingly against the emergence of the macroeconomic expert. And it is against the macroeconomic reasoning of the expert that business, labor, and classical government, all three representing "microeconomics," see themselves as the representatives of one consistent "system of economics," i.e., the competitive system.[21]

LEGISLATING NEOLIBERALISM

There is a tendency inherent in the economic policy of the West German government which seems to apply to all governments within an "industrialized mass society."[22] A postliberalist trend, to which even an allegedly "neoliberalist" government has to pay attention, becomes visible. When the former Ministry of Public

Housing Construction was renamed "Ministry for Spatial Order, etc.," or the Ministry of Labor, "Ministry for Social Order," or when the Ministry of Economics issues commands regarding the foreign exchange rate to be executed by a central bank which legally was established as independent, it is clear that after World War II the government could not limit its economic actions to the global control of over-all *processes* and discredit all specific interventions into the *structure* of the economy as merely partial "adjustment" and "transitional" measures. It has to take into consideration the economic whole, or economic interrelations in their entirety. And that means that the government, as well as any individual politician, must have a concept of what this is or ought to be.

We have seen that West German governments have been reproached for not achieving consistency in their economic actions. We should add that they have been reproached at least as often for not producing a meaningful concept of economic policy. When this reproach was made, for example, in connection with the "energy policy" (the regulation of coal, oil, gas, and atomic energy) of the Erhard administration, there was an undertone of resentment against too much "laissez faire" even from those who were collaborators in principle. Erhard could still reply that, in this special case, all his actions were meant as transitional measures "to lead the coal industry back to the normalcy of the market" after so long a period of protection. But critics from the coal industry and others answered that neither oil nor atomic energy formed what could accurately be called a normal market.

The demand for a conceptually clear economic policy indicates a considerable deviation from old or new principles of economic liberalism. The basic creed of both types of liberalism is that government should not have any ideas on the "economic whole," or, in neoliberalist language, the market structure.[23] The government should limit itself to the will of the "political whole," which it should formulate, express in legal terms, and then execute. Classically, state and government functions thus were restricted to foreign affairs, armed forces, police, schools, hospitals, universities, prisons, law courts, and their respective staffing and financing. The neoliberalist tries to add some "market and growth regulations" and legislation to safeguard competition while maintaining the principle of leaving the economic process to itself.

That this picture is inconsistent with the demand for an economic policy concept is admitted in West Germany, if not by economists, then at least by jurists. The prevailing school of administrative law speaks of *Daseinsvorsorge* (care for private well-being) as an additional, important function of modern government. It has also developed special juridical instruments to carry it out, such as the *Massnahmegesetz* (legal measures), which differ from the classical "law" (Gesetz) in being neither neutral, nondiscriminatory, nor universal but nevertheless are written and passed by the legislative branch (*Gesetzgebung*).[24]

Moreover, the nature of the legislature as a whole has been changing. The parliaments are no longer assemblies of political citizens and their representatives who, according to Burke and other political scientists, "represent the whole nation" and obey only their conscience. They have increasingly become markets where delegates of special interest groups meet in order to trade their services. The services may be of a political nature, but they are, nevertheless, commercialized. They involve monetary transfers effected by public methods, such as by majority vote or tax regulations, but they are designed to satisfy private needs which cannot be filled through the free market.

Thus the demand of the champions of programing and planning for a postliberal economic policy ironically leads to a victory of old-time economic principles in the political institutions. While it is said that the market cannot be left to pure commercial principles, parliament itself develops into a sort of market.

In West Germany, it is the present Chancellor and former Minister of Economics, mainly responsible for the reliberalization of the economy, who himself began complaining about the *"Interessentenhaufen"* ("heap of interestmongers") into which he saw the West Germans develop. In 1965, Erhard launched the concept of the "integrated society" (*Formierte Gesellschaft*) to counteract the individualistic or pluralistic results of his own economic policy. He had already backtracked with his "moderating appeals" to business and labor alike, asking them *not* "to take what the traffic will bear."[25] The West Germans are "an economy in search of a nation," as a British periodical put it.

The explanation of this perplexing mixture of a postliberal economy despising its newly evolved market-like state machine while strongly supporting a neoliberalism economic creed is this: the German people lived for a much longer time than other nations with a government apparatus which was considered a kind of neutral power ruling over the competitive forces of society. But they had had inexorably to learn that it is an illusion. Neither Kaiser nor bureaucracy, state official nor officer of noble origin, administrative jurist nor even member of parliament "representing the whole of the nation" can be considered a "neutral" *tertium* above or aside from the competitive forces of society. All of these are themselves partial interest groups. The Weimar period from 1919 to 1933 already began this lesson, but the majority of Germans clung to the myth of a neutral governing corps. Now, after 1948, they can no longer disregard the fact that they are not governed by a benevolent group of neutral experts, but themselves, and that means by as many partial, private interest groups as make up the society. Parliament has become a reflection of competitive forces; "state" or "society" has become "pluralistic," according to the favorite term used by political scientists and administrative lawyers alike.[26]

The acknowledgment of a commercialized government machinery has a decisive bearing on the discussion of neoliberalist and postliberalist economic policy. Almost every economic policy measure can be presented *both* as favoring a special interest group *and* as serving the economic whole. This discriminating effect of economic legislation pertains even to purely "neutral," "universal," or "global" laws which make a neoliberalist's heart rejoice. Any sort of "reliberalization" certainly damages those interests which profited from the superseded legal structure (e.g., tenants under rent control).[27]

As a consequence, any piece of legislation, be it of a reliberalizing, deliberalizing, newly protective or other nature, arouses the deep concern of all interest groups involved, irrespective of who introduces the bill. All these interest groups will try to get their fair share of a special piece of legislation, in the last instance by voting or abstaining. This is effective even with minorities; it suffices that they can act as a veto group or become a necessary portion of a majority. Thus, on the federal level in West Germany, some important economic or social bills have been passed only by presenting them in a "package," i.e., combining enough attractive material into one bill to secure the required majority from heterogeneous groups of voters.

All this means that it not only pays, but that it is vital to organize as an interest group and to press for legislation, if only to prevent discriminatory government interventions initiated by competitors. All those groups who for one reason or another cannot or do not want to organize as political pressure groups will fall behind economically.

Any political fight which has economic consequences (and which fight hasn't in an industrialized society?) will end with a decision reached by "compromise." Compromise is being introduced as a kind of "new" political method.[28] But what is termed political compromise is, in most cases, the result of a "deal" which does not in the least differ from a deal agreed upon by two businessmen.[29]

This situation substantially wrecks any attempts to pursue a true liberalist economic policy of setting only rules and global targets and executing them by neutral measures leaving intact the price mechanism. It falsifies the results of any remnants of that policy.[30] And, what is most crucial in the context of our study, the commercialization of political administration and legislation not only acts as a check on a policy of liberalism designed to safeguard the commercial principle, it seems to present a much stronger check on any attempt to organize, coordinate, or plan the economic processes.

The final outcome of any global piece of economic legislation within the framework of such a market economy remains uncertain until the very end when the law is passed. The "price," so to speak, remains a matter of chance. And this has to be maintained when the economic *and* political system wants to remain commercial. Compromise in liberalist politics is a necessary instrument.

When, on the other hand, a commercialized parliament wants to pass a piece of economic legislation which aims at planning a partial (or substantial) sector of the economy, it may do so only under the assumption that the economic "program" passed is meant as "indicative" only. Even then its "psychological" (speculative) effect may cause concern. For those who are sure that the program envisaged could only be executed on the basis of their economic loss, ruin, or extinction, even this psychological effect may be intolerable, and the negative vote which they—surely—will cast does not simply bear the mark of an ordinary political "opposition." It may acquire the character of a "resistance" movement. Under such circumstances compromise in postliberal politics may be an impossible instrument.

This becomes all the more aggravating when a political body passes a piece of legislation not only to set signposts but to attain its targets by executive action, e.g., credit policy. By this, the "invisible hand of the market," as Adam Smith called it, becomes visible: it is assumed by executive forces. In other words, the economic entities or even whole sectors which are doomed to shrink will not only know that in advance; they will know how it will be done. And, most significantly, they or their political representatives are asked to cast their vote on the issue. Quite naturally, they will cast this vote in their role of interest representatives and not as guardians of the economic whole who thereby agree to the curtailment of their business as the price of economic progress.

This holds true for programs covering the entire economy or its framework (*Rahmenprogramme*), and it holds true for forecasts and actions pertaining to partial sectors of the economy. Any specific measure (*gezielte Massnahme*) will be regarded as favoring one group and discriminating against another, and will therefore be, even if not meant to, "directed to the slot of the ballot box."[31] With the commercialization of political bodies accomplished to the degree that now exists in West Germany, neither a liberalist nor an interventionist economic policy can escape this reproach. What has resulted from intervention in West Germany until now is mostly not the reflection of any party or parliamentarian or government forethought, not the result of any premeditated, coherent program or plan, but the hazardous outcome of a purely unplanned majority, a veto group, or a coalition-compromise situation. "You are quite right," said the Secretary of State of the Ministry of Labor and Social Order to the champion of a liberalist economic policy, "you are always right, but I keep telling you, you will never get a majority."[32]

It is possible that, things being as they are, it is the neoliberalist creed which appears once more, having completed a full circle, to be the best solution. If any economic policy measure is doomed to fall into the trap of conflicting interests, it would be best to abstain as much as possible from any intervention and return to the "self-regulating forces of the market." This is indeed a recommendation often heard and acclaimed—especially since the inequalities of the starting point in 1948 (or 1933, or 1923, or the nineteenth century) fade away and since the inequalities arising from the present competitive struggle no longer inflict great injury due to the raising of the average income to a level where great poverty is unknown even to the back-benchers of success.

One could sum up this sketch of economic policy carried on in the Federal Republic as follows: There are many government interventions enacted by political forces into, or even against, the allegedly "self-regulating market forces." But, whereas in times of "archliberalism" such interventions were made "for others," by a "benevolent, neutral" government, or by a responsible liberal bourgeoisie assenting to *"sozialpolitik"* as an act of grace or undisputed leadership, nowadays such interventions are made *"for* others *by* others," or not infrequently *by* the bourgeoisie *for* themselves (e.g., subsidies). The result is that economic policy can no longer be differentiated from social policy.

But this does not mean that legislating is carried out within the context of a clearly defined *social* policy objective such as "harmonious growth including adjustment assistance to lame ducks." It means, quite the contrary, that social policy is carried out in many cases as the outcome of the *economic* principle of monopolistic competition raised to the square power and lifted from the market to the parliamentary level. If there might have been any other integrating principle but competition inherent in *Soziale Marktwirtschaft* or neoliberalism, it certainly did not become the dominating principle in West Germany.

✝✝✝✝✝✝✝✝✝✝✝✝✝✝✝✝✝✝✝✝ **IV** ✝✝✝✝✝✝✝✝✝✝✝✝✝✝✝✝✝✝✝✝✝✝

Men and Their Motives:
The Sociological Scene

"The leading types" to be described here make up the Establishment in politics and economics: owner-entrepreneurs, nonowner business managers, directors and staff members of interest organizations (including farmers), labor unions, higher civil servants, party and parliament leaders, financial leaders (including private bankers), managers of great banks, and majority stockholders in big corporations. With the exception of, perhaps, church leaders, journalists, and university professors, there are no other social types exerting any influence in the stream of affairs in the Bonn Republic.

This is a phenomenon which could not be stated with conviction until very recently. Leaders of interest organizations and even of parties and parliaments occupied a subordinate rank until very late in the twentieth century, while the civil service functioned as a simple executing device. Among the types predominating socially until World War I were the princely houses, the landowning gentry, and the Army and Navy officers' corps. Exceptions were to be found in the Hanseatic cities and in some southwestern parts of the Second Reich. Even during the Weimar Republic remnants of these once established strata of society managed to retain their influence. It is only now, after the second total military defeat of the Reich, that the leaders of business, labor, associations, parties, parliaments, and state officialdom find themselves "on top" or "in front" without the former "elites" competing with them. The situation is new, and the feeling of taking full responsibility for political and economic affairs has still to be gradually internalized.

Owner-Entrepreneurs

According to the legitimacy doctrine as reformulated after 1948–49, it is the private businessman who is the backbone of a society organized around the free competitive market. In West Germany, the "secondary sector" (according to Colin Clark) is still dominating development, though the tertiary sector is gaining in importance as the area where input of new techniques, in machinery as well as in management, will produce high profits.[1]

One can take it for granted that the vast numerical majority of all industrial firms (though not a vast majority of the money volume or of employed labor), falls within the category *"selbständige Unternehmer,"* i.e., industrialists who manage *and* own their business, either individually or as family property. Because of the degree of concentration reached in Germany, this may not amount to a large share of the market. But their sociological importance is not negligible. Besides, one must remember that, though 75 per cent of all enterprises are small (with less than fifty employees), and though owner-entrepreneurs predominantly originate from this mass, there are still many medium-sized and some large industrial firms in Germany which, whether organized as a family company or as a *Kapitalgesellschaft* (stockholding or limited liability company) are owned by a family or belong to individuals like Bosch, Krupp, Voith (Heidenheim), and others. There are still individual big businessmen who represent the "caste."

Since World War I and with redoubled efforts since World War II there have been attempts to wipe out the distinction between owner-industrialist and manager-industrialist. Nowadays, the term *Unternehmer* (entrepreneur), strictly speaking, applies to both. In the language of nineteenth-century economics, the word referred to the function of (rather than the man) bringing together resources, material, labor, and capital.[2]

Official language still tends to stress the fact that an *Unternehmer* is anyone who works and is responsible for the combination of men, material, and money within the market; but there has crept in a tendency to see the "true entrepreneur" as one who, in addition to being manager, is responsible for his own capital. The distinction between "personal, liable" capital versus "anonymous, stock" capital (with the latter no longer very different from long-term, fixed-interest loans[3]) tends to stay *en vogue*. This distinction receives additional support from the fact that owner-entrepreneurs are usually limited to the problems of small business, whereas manager-entrepreneurs represent big business.

The idea that small business is owned and big business administered is reflected by professional and interest groups. The *Arbeitsgemeinschaft Selbständiger Unternehmer* (Association of Independent Entrepreneurs) was founded after World War II to represent the "independents," i.e., owner-entrepreneurs in trade and industry. But because of its actions and publications it is generally accepted as representing small business.[4]

At any rate, the idea that the philosophy of the owner-entrepreneur is the truest expression of *Soziale Marktwirtschaft* has dominated—if not official language—official use and action. Most top representatives of business associations, professional groups, and semiofficial bodies (such as the Federation of Industries, the Management Association, and Chambers of Commerce) are elected from among the "independent" (and mostly small) businessmen, even in those regions (such as the Ruhr area) in which large stockholding enterprises are definitely dominant.

The target of the second phase of *Soziale Marktwirtschaft* was proclaimed during the 1957 election campaign by Erhard's party (CDU)[5] to be "people's capitalism," everyone an "owner" in some way, including holding shares or even a savings account. This may mean something quite different from owning or managing a business, and that the "owners" have a share in the productive capital of the economy is regarded as making them full members of society. The less than 100,000 persons who represent ownership and management of "private industry," even if supported by the more than 750,000 artisans, the 1.7 million farmers and the hundreds of thousands of professionals and retailers may consider themselves far from the "ideal man." But despite the complaint sometimes heard that the West Germans are becoming "a people of employees," it is the industrial owner-entrepreneur, his sons and heirs, who are being pushed into the foreground.

Who is he? First of all, he is much better known as "a function" than as a person or even an image. This stratum of society has failed most lamentably in doing a job of public relations.[6] Yet if we look behind the functional screen and beyond the individual differences which cloak the essential traits of a group, we may note certain distinguishing characteristics. The most easily discerned types have been the old ones and the young ones, or grandfathers and grandsons. The in-between generation of sons or fathers, born between 1905 and 1929, if still alive after losses from terror and war, is more difficult to describe. Yet each of these displays marked character traits.

Grandfathers have rebuilt their factories, rallied the consent and confidence of the workers, and recaptured customers and markets. They bridged the gap between 1933 (or even 1929) and 1948. They remembered the Great Depression and unemployment, Hitler's employment campaign and the tightening of the planning screw when Stalingrad changed the course of the war. But they also remembered the function of credit and exchange bills, remembered customers in foreign countries, free money transfer, and world trade. Above all, they could remember the sovereign feeling of a royal merchant, the philosophy of a private fortune and liable capital. There was a dangerous abyss to bridge, when entirely unorthodox methods of financing were applied to form capital after the 1948 currency reform. Self-financing, anticipated by short-term bank loans invested for long terms, caused sleepless nights. But the boom justified this unroyal merchant device. By 1960 the philosophy of the grandfathers largely returned to that of the 1927 period, or even, some say, 1912, with the noises of two world wars, the Great Depression, two inflations, and cold war sounding like remote thunderstorms passing by or fading away. The right, privilege, and safety of private property is restored. Naturally, one has to defend it against attempts to "plan it away" and to be on guard against any form of "cold socialization" like French planning—but radical open attacks against private property and its economic order have become obsolete even among Social Democrats.

It is among these grandfathers of private business where one could find, and still does find, the advocates of cartel practice. It is they who argue that one cannot—as was attempted with the 1957 Anticartel Law—outlaw cartelizing without striking at mergers and natural growth. They demand revision of the Anticartel Law. They demand *Verbandsdemokratie* aimed at increasing the opportunities for small business to influence pressure group decisions. They demand abolition of laws fostering concentration, such as the

German system of turnover taxes and corporation income taxes by which the largest firms enhance their opportunities to increase capital by self-financing, whereas the capital "cushion" of small private business is lamentably small. In demanding the abolition of discrimination, these older representatives of independent business sometimes go so far as to demand new discriminatory measures that will this time work in their favor.

The "grandsons," who now more and more take the reins of the family firms, have watched their grandfathers rebuild the economy. They have little or no memory dating back from 1945 to 1929. They take the interrelationship of institutions such as parliamentary democracy, market economy, free enterprise, and private property for granted—much more so than their grand-fathers who, at any rate, know other ways from experience. They do not try to separate politics from economics, but what they do— and here they part from their grandfathers—is to search for a new legitimating principle for the whole institutional setup.

Usually this takes the form of demanding a modern justification for private property as an inherited right. The conventions and periodicals of "Young Entrepreneurs" (*Junge Unternehmer*)[7] are full of debates on the principle of private property, all steadfastly defending the principle of free enterprise and market economy against socialist or bureaucratic intervention or planning. By quite logical reasoning, they go so far as to anticipate the shrinking, even bankruptcy, of their fathers' or their own businesses if structural or cyclical events so demand. Thus they acknowledge the market system, but they search for a justification of their own heritage, i.e., for their own place within this system.

Not so the grandfathers. What makes them insecure is not a shaking of belief in their role in the *economic* system but a loss of their political platform. It is they who mainly abstained from engaging in active politics as long as they lived; their political creed expressed itself, on various occasions, in a simple belief—moderate or excessive—in nationalism and "fulfilling one's duty to the father-land." Beyond the limits of their own business, they accept the political myths of nation, state, fatherland, and people and their representatives, with no intermediary agents such as interest groups, ministries, or political parties.

It is here that the marked difference between grandfathers and grandsons is to be found. While their economic philosophies may still be much alike, in politics they deviate. The young businessmen engage in practical party and pressure group work so long as they can afford the time, i.e., before they have taken the management of the company in their hands, and even after. And they work at the grass roots level of local diets and Länder parliaments, leaving (until recently) national issues in the federal parliament to others. For the young, the myths of nation, state, and fatherland mean little. What matter are structures, functions, mechanisms, institutions, and people. What does not matter to them, and what they tend to overlook, are the power of traditions, the inertia of human groups, and the trans-technical effort which men have to exert to overcome both tradition and inertia and establish something new.

Both grandsons and grandfathers resist change. The grandsons do not even conceive of changing things from the roots. They do not understand people who try to do so, e.g., the Bolshevist planners. A campaign slogan invented by the Christian Democrats during the 1957 election expressed admirably this sentiment shared for different reasons by old and young—"No experiments!" (*Keine Experimente*).

Here we see the difference between grandfathers and grandsons on the one side and what is left of the "father" or "son" generation on the other. The "father-sons" do not trust the quiet of the surface; they know how radical changes come about. They have witnessed at least one, often two or three, radical changes of character and belief in their fathers (the grandfathers); they know how deep one has to dig to find the unchangeable essence of a man.

Their prevalent feeling is that everything is provisional, and, hence, there is an excuse for treachery of all sorts. The majority of the sons (and sons-in-law, we might add) has settled for a good life with little concern beyond the actions indispensable for securing it. As a hobby, this majority might engage in "watching" events, preferably as an "inside-dopester";[8] they usually are keen observers and, if sufficiently able, remorseless thinkers. But they shun action, make good second men or staff people, and if—which has to happen with an heir to private property—they are chosen first men, they are unwilling to assume authority. If they are assigned leadership of any sort, they take it up *contre coeur*. Naturally there are exceptions.[9]

To sum up this brief and subjective social psychology of entre-preneurs in West Germany after 1948:

(1) The older generation has helped, in the leading role assigned to it, to reconstruct a business community by practical action. It does little in reflecting on how to fortify this community intellectually and politically against potential enemies. This remains the task of authorities beyond the oldsters' everyday concern.

(2) The younger generation has learned its practices from the older one. It wants to continue these practices as inherited, but it also wants to participate actively in their intellectual and political protection. It thinks that in doing so it simply has to transfer to the fields of politics, administration, and mass media, the skill, knowledge, and techniques as learned and applied in business practice.

(3) The middle generation (what is left of it) wants to muddle through without sticking its neck out. It knows the unsurmountable dividing lines between technology, psychology, and politics. It knows that the boss cannot keep a mass strike from developing into a mass riot by technical tricks or by psychological knowledge that can be taught, but only by presenting himself (on screen or in the factory courtyard) and speaking words other than those used in business negotiations. And this generation expects mass strikes and mass riots during its lifetime. But it does not want to be boss. Nor does it aspire to become the teacher. Some of its saddest specimens live by the slogan: *"nous, après le déluge"* (meaning "survival first").

NONOWNER MANAGERS

In comparative studies and observations, two features are usually mentioned as being characteristic of German business executives: the emphasis on business as a "vocation" rather than a profession and the "greatest resistance to the nonowner manager."[10] One might think that it is the heirs of family enterprises who insist that they have been "chosen," rather than the hired managers (a term which still carries a somewhat derogatory connotation).

This is definitely not the case. One could argue, on the contrary, that it is the top executives, nonowners, of large and medium-sized corporations who insist on the need to "have a touch" for the speculative side of business, who are in some way seeking chosen people with the grace-of-the-market sign as potential successors (*Führungskräfte-Nachwuchs*), while still asking for solid, acquired knowledge and trained experience as a second leg to stand on. The heir of an owner-entrepreneur will usually be much more cautious in invoking vocation and grace than the top manager of a corporation looking for his "heir."[11]

Perhaps the "salaried executive," as the French call him, needs the distinction of vocation and grace to substitute for the divine right of property which he lacks. He needs it more than the property heir who has—or at least had—his principle of legitimacy. To discard any distinguishing characteristics for top managers of individual firms is dangerous in a society which sees itself as organized around the free competition of businessmen. There is, for example, a marked tendency not to overstress effort or efficiency (*Leistung*) as qualifying a top manager, for this criterion is an entirely formalistic one and applies as well to a foreman or a laboratory engineer as to the executive board of responsible managers.

The common denominator of owner and nonowner manager is the notion of risk-taking and risk-bearing, a function well justified within the system of a market society, though originally it applied only to risking one's own capital. A manager who has no share of his company's capital will answer, when questioned about the risk he takes, that he risks his good name. If told that this is true for every citizen in all kinds of professions, he will specify that his name is connected with a special, unique gift: that of coordinating men, material, machines, and money in order to produce profit in a market.[12]

It is true that this attitude will be colored and scaled according to many environmental conditions. It may depend upon whether it is expressed by the salaried executive of a family firm or by the head of a stockholding company with 300,000 shareholders, or whether we talk to managers residing in a highly commercialized and merchant-governed Hanseatic city, or in small business districts such as Württemberg or Sauerland, or whether we interview the top executive of a Ruhr steel mill.

While salaried managers may express different views about government subsidies for individual firms or for whole sectors,[13] they are practically united in their steadfast defense of a market economy with no over-all coordination (planning) of *individual* economic movements by governmental forces. They are also united in their tense refusal to have private property rights curtailed any more. They know it is the very principle of private property which gives them their independence as salaried top managers, especially when voting shareholders are scattered in the thousands. The only controls they formally recognize are the "forces of the market," including the capital market; any curtailment of property rights would necessitate the introduction of other forms of control.[14] The Law on Co-Determination for Coal and Steel and, to a lesser degree, the Law on Factory Councils, mentioned earlier, have already brought about quite a heavy curtailment of property rights.[15] It is the salaried managers who are, privately, quite dissatisfied with this development and oppose vigorously any extension of the Co-Determination Law.

The Co-Determination Law has made compulsory for all coal and steel producing stockholding companies the institution of a "Labor Director," a full member of the top executive board (*Vorstand*)—to be distinguished from the top *supervisory* body (*Aufsichtsrat*) which by the same law is packed with 50 per cent workers' delegates. This labor director is voted into office—like all the other top executives—with the participation of the 50 per cent labor votes in the supervising body. In addition, he is proposed by the workers themselves, which practically means by the union dominating the firm's employees. Oddly enough, the law emphasizes the responsibility of this creature of labor to the regular organs of the stockholding company. The labor director, as a member of the executive board, is obliged to work for the good of the company (not only of the workers) and can be held responsible by the Aufsichtsrat.

Thus, corporate board members have a managing colleague who is a member in full right, but whose allegiance to rigid market principles has not yet been ascertained in emergency cases and who cannot be counted on to stay loyal to free competition in times of crisis. Still, this man legally and socially is a "manager," i.e., a member of the top executive board of a business. And what is more important, he has not been nominated and elected by capital, but by capital plus labor, and in most instances he is by social origin and family background a workman or employee.

Opposition to this institution of a "new management" has, to our present knowledge, been even stronger among "classical" managers chosen by capital alone than among owners themselves— even though the latter were partially dispossessed by this reduction in their voting power, while the rights of the former remained formally untouched. This strong opposition may be explained by the classical managers' fear that, by adding a labor member to their board, the impression may be created that "managing" an industrial business is not a matter of gifted people operating with risk and good luck amidst the competitive forces of the market but may be trusted to anybody, even one of a proletarian or socialist origin.

This question of social or intellectual origin becomes all the more important when we consider the educational qualifications of a manager. Special, intense training by universities, institutes of technology, or post-university management training centers is considered more and more a necessary prerequisite for a high managerial post. Since such training is open to more or less all people above a certain intelligence level,[16] the "professional" side of a manager's training is no longer helpful in establishing the distinction required as a substitute for private property. Union officials (usually those who will later staff the business boards as labor directors), social democrats, and bureaucrats are now getting an academic background similar to that of the salaried business executives. Their training may include law, business, economics, technology, or the natural sciences. It is significant, however, that self-made or non-academic managers are still widely found.

Thus, an aspiring manager cannot count on excelling by a high degree of specialization obtained inside or outside the universities, or by any kind of "professionalizing" experience. What is asked for is "generalization"—or "specialization in generalities"—rather than expert knowledge and practice.[17] This specialization in being a generalist, however, is a double-edged knife; one has to be careful not to be loyal to so general a cause that one becomes a security risk for an individual firm. For example, economists are believed to make bad businessmen (though they may become good state officials), and two special groups of managers who entered business after World War II are still not accepted on a fully equal level by the old foxes. To these belong most men of the "son" generation. They had their training during the Third Reich either in one or more of the many corporate estates, or they switched from Army officer (mostly with general staff training) to business executive. Some men in these two groups have in the meantime reached the president's level in their firms, but it still remains uncertain which way they will steer in times of crisis, when survival is not a matter of organizational routine alone.

This "son" generation is now reaching the stage of taking over from the grandfather generation of managers. The grandsons in this echelon of nonowner managers are still in the specializing stage at the age of thirty-five or below. As for the grandfathers, it is they who (often pushed to the foreground by the owners who, as in France, did not want to dirty their hands) navigated through the Nazi period, cooperating as necessary with politicians and immoral elements in order to keep their business afloat. Some of them have been in office from the Big Depression through National Socialism until the peak of post-war reconstruction.[18]

From them, the "sons" take over much more cautiously than do the grandsons in family firms and politics. Since they are prudent in their public statements, including those directed to their shareholders and supervisory board members, any judgment of their dogmatism or lack of dogmatism, especially pertaining to economic structure, seems premature. What can be said is that until 1963 German business was still shaped by the grandfather generation. There are, of course, exceptions.

What remains of the characterizing features of the German business "oligarchy"[19] of old times is an attempt to counterbalance the egalitarian effect of "professionalizing the calling" by providing personal contacts among deputy managers and the ruling generation. Based upon the general mistrust of university training for business, industry has created its own centers for training middle, upper, and top executives in post-university and mid-career seminars.[20] "Training," in most instances, is quite different from the Anglo-Saxon or French model. There is no teaching staff but only "exchange of experience" among top managers and deputy executives.

But the underlying reason for these meetings seems to be less the transfer of knowledge and experience than the formation of a "spirit of likemindedness." The kernel of this spirit of likemindedness is the common understanding of leadership in a business society. Attempts are made to base this understanding on practical experience rather than dogmatic or systematic insight. "Training for mastering tomorrow's progress" might summarize this training pattern.

The author doubts, from his own experience, whether this training will mature within the limit prescribed by the grandfathers: namely, that change and progress have to remain restricted to technological, scientific, organizational, and psychological alterations within a business society of market individuals competing for money rewards. There is no reason why the managers of tomorrow, if the need arises, should not change the very rules of the system too.

INTEREST ASSOCIATIONS: DIRECTORS AND STAFF MEMBERS

The leading role of the owner or nonowner businessman is reflected outside the firms and corporations by the semi-political associations in the "pre-parliamentarian field." These organizations of industry and management, of the chambers of commerce, of farmers, of trade, and of craftsmen have a political status sometimes surpassing even their economic significance. Moreover, the businessman's prestige also shows in the often limited influence of the permanent secretaries and the other staff personnel within these organizations. Policies are clearly shaped by members of the directing boards and sometimes not even exclusively executed by the full-time secretaries. Even with those pressure groups which are predominantly composed of nonowner managers of industry, a new line is drawn, distinguishing between a nonowner who runs a business and one who only runs a *Verband* (interest organization).

The alleged difference is artificially maintained, as may be inferred from the fact that, within the scope of these associations, both businessman and association executive—one as president or vice president, the other as general secretary—try to exert political influence and, by this influence, try to improve the structural or cyclical situation of their industry or sector.[21]

This means that such interest associations are usually inactive in maintaining and defending the free play of the market. Often, quite to the contrary, they introduce additional mechanisms for money transfers by government. This action, of course, is often accompanied by strong proclamations supporting economic liberalism, the right of private property, and the maintenance of free competition.

Some of these interest organizations stem from before World War I. Most of them profited from a much enhanced prestige when the National Socialists turned them (or their predecessors or substitutes) into semi-official state cartels executing an economic policy which, by ingenious design, combined profit with security. Some pressure groups still carry on according to this philosophy. Examples are the Farmers' League (*Bauernverband*) or the Organized Artisans. Some of these organizations have increased their prestige and power with the postwar boom which multiplied the earnings of participating firms, notably the Federation of German Industries (*Bundesverband der Deutschen Industrie*, BDI), or the Organization of Private Banking. Here, too, we find the familiar phenomenon of these organizations seeking to elect a president to represent them in public who is an owner-manager rather than the nonowner manager of their most powerful firm.

We have to add here that the associations of West German business have a two-pronged organizational structure. First, all firms are grouped by economic sectors (industry and its branches, agriculture, craftsmen, liberal professions, trade, etc.). Secondly, they are also organized as "management" (*Arbeitgeber*) and again split up according to sectors. It is these management associations which act as parties in collective bargaining with the unions, not sectoral organizations.

This organizational structure, in addition to masking real relations, also results in a considerable and unnecessary inflation of presidential, secretarial, and staff personnel. Indeed, the situation is complicated by two additional forms of differentiation. In accordance with the federal structure of the Federal Republic, all organizations are split up in local and Länder subgroupings, the latter carrying full autonomy of action. Finally, there are also the cross-sectional, semi-official chambers of commerce, trade, farmers, and artisans associations, and so forth.

It goes without saying that it is difficult to find enough competent people to lead and to staff all these organizations. Few secretaries fulfill important functions, and not all positions are, therefore, aspired to by keen young people. Mostly, secretaries and staff are trained academic economists or jurists who did not, or did not want to, make their way inside business firms and corporations, either because they had become "too generalized," or they had recognized that they were not tough enough for the competitive life.

Another consequence of the organizational structure of business and management in Germany is, simply, that the other side is organized the same way. Hence, there are sixteen labor unions organized according to the "industry" principle, and each of these sixteen is broken up, once more, according to the federal structure of the Republic, into eleven autonomous Länder organizations (not counting regional and local units). It is the Länder level which takes part in collective bargaining. The central federal secretariat, with staff, president, and secretary, is much less powerful than those who do the bargaining. Again, just as with management, it is difficult to staff all these positions. Some branch union leaders indulge in the costly luxury of building their own staff structure which practically duplicates the one at the top level.

In addition, the "unity union" principle by which, in 1949, the former rival unions of Weimar (Socialist, Christian, and cooperative) were joined together, did not work out in all respects. There are, at least, two rival union organizations competing with the unity union: *Deutsche Angestellton Gewerkschaft* (DAG), a white collar union; and a Christian union (CGD), now defunct.

Oddly enough, the suspicion displayed by business managers toward their social equals, the managers of associations, is evidenced in the trade unions too. There exists a marked distrust of "eggheads" and intellectuals, experts and consultants who do not stem from the rank and file of workers and employees, even if these technicians are badly needed and dedicated, loyal unionists, even socialists. This explains why those with academic training have not yet passed the consultant stage in shaping the policies and thoughts of labor unions in West Germany.

With the retirement from active duty of the old union leaders who were already active before 1933, when Hitler outlawed the labor movement, the workers' organization had to look and plan for new leaders. Labor was in a slightly different position than that of capital and management. The latter continued in some way through the totalitarian Third Reich; their old men were able to conserve at least their basic skills and to produce successors. Not so with the labor union movement. The National Socialist "Workers' Front" (*Arbeitsfront*) was something entirely different; there one could not learn how to organize a strike, for instance. Striking was forbidden.

One could argue that lockouts, too, were forbidden; hence the younger generation of entrepreneurs also had no chance to learn important skills.[22] But the manager of a company has other, equally vital, responsibilities in his role as a manager. A union leader gains prominence only by skillful bargaining with the "partner."

In addition, German labor unions have not, since Marxian times, contented themselves with raising the money income of their members. They felt a higher duty to fight for and protect the basic human rights of the worker. It was a kind of attenuated Marxism which was the life blood of the German labor movement from its beginning up to revival in the 1950's.

It is not easy to educate people in this spirit once the tradition has been interrupted for at least twelve years. Special schools and training centers have been built for union members. But it seems as if the rank and file of the unions today are interested in other things than the lesson of the "Weimar experience." If capitalist business and liberal government proved incompetent to overcome the unemployment crisis in 1930, the unions of that time, with their claims for economic democracy and human rights, showed no greater ability to rise to power, provide work, and, later, prevent Hitler from gaining power. Therefore, between 1950 and 1962 union leaders turned away from their former high aims, even from the socialist reform program so successfully begun with the Co-Determination Law in 1951. They behaved like tough "Americanized" pressure groups fighting for higher wages, jealously guarding their rights to bargain collectively and to strike.[23] They, too, were sworn to basically loyal acceptance of the market principle. Competing for money through collective bargaining is above all else an outgrowth of free competition.

This holds true even when it could no longer be said to be "atomistic competition"; the "countervailing powers" of management and labor are officially recognized as compatible with *Soziale Marktwirtschaft* by Constitution and law. Their organizations are exempted *expressis verbis* from the effect of the Anticartel Law.

It is the "son" generation of labor which seems to question the liberalist solution for "wage fights," at the same time distrusting Marxian precepts. On the one hand, Georg Leber, president of the construction workers' union, a most potent though small group working in a booming industry, tried to establish a kind of new cooperative mechanism between labor and management which is not meant to replace fights but which tries to combine both elements into a kind of "common responsibility for industry as a whole." Leber's attempt was executed half-heartedly; there was strong opposition on the part of other unions as well as among entrepreneurs themselves. On the other hand, the formidable metal workers' union, led by the dynamic Otto Brenner, and other powerful unions started to press again for extension of co-determination into industries other than coal and steel. They thereby reactivated in 1964–65 a slogan which had never been taken off the union program.

At present, with the postwar boom attentuated, the majority of union leaders still seem to enjoy a neoliberalist phase of union policy which brings them more and more returns in the form of higher wages. Bills which aim toward some regulation of wage fights by a mechanism "consistent with the market" (hence with union autonomy) are turned down, even if similar regulations have already been agreed upon through collective bargaining or are later negotiated.[24] Unions seem to remain loyal followers of the neoliberalist Chancellor Erhard just as they were in 1957 when they supported the Anticartel Law against the vote of many businessmen or supported the independence of the Central Bank from political intervention.[25]

CIVIL SERVANTS

Until recently, public administration in Germany bore the mark of the nineteenth century, even of absolutist times. Two distinguishing features are indicative of this. First, the public service corps is divided into "lower," "middle," with the subdivision "upper middle," and "higher" services. It is the higher service which largely staffs the important positions in Land and Federal ministries. An academic training is, with rare exceptions, a basic prerequisite for the higher service.

Secondly, it is only very slowly that the lawyers' monopoly in the higher service begins to give way to other forms of training. That a high government official had to be a jurist is a direct consequence of the circumstances under which the "state" in Europe was born and developed. Administration was regarded as an activity which (in a monarchy) cast into legal form, and (in a democracy) executed, the legal will of the sovereign, first of a king, then of a parliament. This interpretation of the government was strengthened by the economic liberalism of the nineteenth century. The "Rechtsstaat" (rule of law) became more and more a "Gesetzesstaat" (rule of acts). It had to become so, for this was the only legal instrument considered compatible with a functioning market economy. Legalistic formalism thus suppressed the practical element contained in administration training under the mercantilist tradition.

The decisive difference between the jurists' training and role in the Anglo-Saxon legal tradition and in the Germanic-Romanic law must also be remembered. Germany, like France and other countries, has for centuries followed the Roman Law system, which led to a different concept of the "state" than what is called "government" in England or the United States. It may be true that in recent times this difference, once overestimated, has been reduced to a matter of interpretation rather than organization. But traditions which can be explained only by the Roman Law system still exert a great influence on the German jurist of today and enable him to occupy an important and almost unique place in the administrative system of society.[26] Thus it is the jurists' monopoly that is responsible for another characteristic of the German civil service: its concept of allegiance to the state as "neutral," above conflicting interests, though sometimes personified by either an emperor or a president.[27]

It was these traditions or developments—the withering away of the mercantilist-cameralist knowledge and practice, the rise of the liberalist economic doctrine, and the neutrality principle of civil service interpreted in a special way—which made it an especially difficult task for the German corps of government servants to take into consideration macroeconomic thinking and action.

Three streams of events have worked to mitigate to some extent this hampering concentration of tradition, although it was not until the end of World War II and the foundation of the Bonn Republic that all three of them became operative. First, it was necessary to staff new, "unclassical" ministries which were explicitly concerned with specific economic problems: refugees, water and atomic power, underdeveloped countries, Marshall Plan, housing construction—functions nonexistent before 1919. For these tasks one needs statistics, economics, and even experts on sociology.

Second, there was the vulnerability of administrative positions to a special sort of spoils system serving both parties and interest groups. Conservative advocates of civil service neutrality complain bitterly about this "corruption."[28] But they cannot prevent the practice of representatives of interest groups entering administration after having been labeled "experts" (*Sachverständige*). Indeed, as experts these representatives can even claim to introduce or reintroduce another form of neutrality into government. Under absolutist rule or liberalist law, "expertism" (*Sachverstand*) did not need to be introduced into government via interest groups; it could be bought at universities and was called jurisprudence.

At any rate, it is this background which illuminates and helps one judge the creation of new organs in government administration: the independent boards and the groups and bodies of independent consultants, experts, and scientific councils, sometimes loosely attached to classical ministries or similar offices. Many of the ministries use "Wissenschaftliche Beiräte."[29] Some of these "neutral scientific expert bodies" have been explicitly established by special laws, such as the "Advisory Council on Social Policy" (Sozialbeirat) created on the occasion of the indexing of the social security pension system, or the law creating an Expert Council for Giving Opinions on Over-all Economic Development.

Thirdly, another development which demands economic reasoning of a noncommercial sort from the German civil service is the necessity to provide staff for supranational bodies. It is here that German officials meet with French, Belgian, Italian, British, and American colleagues, negotiating and discussing special questions of economic policy, and it is here that uneasy statements are expressed by politicians, businessmen, and administrators alike. The German negotiators are mostly pushed to the wall by the French. The same French civil service training that in discussions of a more ideological order is castigated as "technocratic" is recognized and acknowledged (if grudgingly) as efficient. Even a formalistic jurist such as Professor Hallstein goes back, upon becoming president of the European Economic Community, to the mercantilist tradition of his profession and "administers" in a way which rouses the fury of his former colleague, Professor Erhard.[30]

But only slowly is the jurists' monopoly being overcome. Reform of university education drags along, and a closer contact between civil service, business, and unions has yet to come about. The international exchange of students and of practicing officials is most promising. Yet it seems that German administration, when called upon to help labor, capital, and management, will always be one step behind foreign civil service practice.

POLITICIANS AND EXPERTS

In 1953 and 1961, the composition of the Federal Parliament by professions and occupations was as follows:[31]

	1953	1961
Officials and employees of government administration and honorary officials	100	120
Lawyers, advocates, business trustees	36	39
Teachers, university professors, ministers, physicians	33	32
Journalists, writers, editors	32	36
Entrepreneurs of industry and commerce	60	59
Business managers	16	17
Retail traders, artisans, and representatives of their pressure groups	35	37
Farmers and farmers' representatives	62	62
Employees and workmen	25	28
Unions' and other employees' organization members, representatives, and members of social security service	59	50
Administrative staff of party organizations	35	33
Housewives	16	13
Total	509	526

It may be interesting to make a breakdown according to age. The average age of the members of the first two parliaments was about fifty, which means that the "average" M.P. was born about 1900 and, therefore, belonged to the "grandfather generation" we described above.

By permission of the Allied Occupation Forces, beginning from 1945–46, parties were allowed to reconstitute on a Länder basis. It was these reborn parties and their personnel that composed the assembly which shaped the "constitution" (called the Basic Law) of the Federal Republic and finally created the Länder Diets and the Bundestag of the new Republic on September 20, 1949.[32]

Considering the date of the re-created parties and the age of the first parliamentarians, we have ample proof of the fact that it was, in the main, the membership of the Reichstag and the Landtage of the Weimar Republic who took up their work again—but not quite in the same spirit. In formulating the constitution, for example, they all agreed not to repeat many Weimarian provisions which they considered deficient: for instance, procedures for a plebiscite or the emergency power of a President. Instead, to insure a stable government, they inserted the "constructive vote of nonconfidence" into the new text. This indeed helped to stabilize Adenauer's government for fourteen years. The first Chancellor was himself representative of Weimar tradition, having been lord mayor of Cologne throughout the twenties and already a public figure of high standing at that time. When he came to the chancellery in 1949 he was seventy-three years of age. But he stood on the platform of a party that had not existed in Weimar, the CDU.

There were other changes in mind and attitude from Weimar to Bonn. There had been imprisonment, emigration, and devastating shocks among the former Reichstag members now in the Bundestag. But there was much continuity. Where else could they have gathered their experience and formed their habits if not in Berlin before 1933? The author remembers a West German party convention in 1957, immediately after the Saarland had been reincorporated into the Federal Republic. There were present, for the first time, representatives of the Saar brethren party organization sent to carry out the merger; these appeared much younger than the average party leader in Bonn. They followed the debates with an air of boredom and an obvious lack of comprehension. It was clear that they did not understand the issue at stake, which was a continuation of some Weimar controversy. The Saar had known no

Weimar period; it had been under League of Nations mandatory rule from 1919 to 1935.

All the new demands combined to operate in the direction of change. After 1949 there was much more detailed work, instead of the over-all political debate required of the ordinary parliamentarian during the Weimar period. With laws encompassing more than one thousand paragraphs and volumes of thousands of pages (e.g., the social security reform, or the Federal Construction Law), the painstaking legislative burden changed parliamentarian existence from "politics" to "labor." In other words, after having been for centuries justified by being a "generalist" (or "specialist in generalities"), the member of parliament had to turn into a specialist, an expert. Lacking a legislative reference service such as U.S. congressmen have, the Bundestag members began to look for a solution.[33]

They responded to that challenge in different ways. First, the representative could look for the help of some "private" reference service, such as the staff work of parties, interest groups, private firms, or other organizations. But this had some evil results. It was practical only for those who already "had connections," and certainly not for backbenchers. The help of outside expert staffs tended, naturally, to color opinions and decisions. The author remembers several party committee debates and decision-forming discussions where a politician backed by "expert help" carried the votes because he alone knew the details of a five-hundred-paragraph law. The expert he had with him was the lawyer of a private firm.

Second, the party machine may try to compose diets and parliaments in such a way that for every specialized field of legislation there is an expert on each slate. This has had alarming effects on the theory and practice of parliament. By introducing a sort of "division of labor" into parliament, it acknowledges that the activity of a member of parliament has become a special sort of work and is no longer "politics" in the classical sense. Also, a party machine must, in order to make up the slate as an "ideal mixture," have the power to select and carry out its choice. This contradicts the classical doctrine of majority vote and election of persons (instead of selection of specialists) by the constituency. The technique of selection does not necessarily have to be provided by the election principle of proportional representation (as is the case in Germany for one-half of the M.P.'s); it can also work with majority vote (as has been discovered in Great Britain).[34] In West Germany, it is true, the introduction of specialists into parliaments is usually done by placing them in "safe" constituencies *and* by placing them on the "Länder Lists" which make up one-half of the representatives selected by the party machine. A "technician" who is, at the same time, a good vote getter in critical constituencies is a rare exception.

It is instructive that party bosses on the federal level (such as the first Chancellor) have complained of the fact that there are only "Land Lists," no "Federal List." In order to get a high-caliber specialist with no vote-pulling power into parliament, federal politicians have to come to terms with regional (Land) party bosses who often have other ideas on who should be given a safe place on the Land List. Adenauer, therefore, has been trying to add a Federalist List to the electoral legislation, but so far in vain.

Third, the representative may withdraw from active participation in parliamentary work, especially from work in highly specialized committees,[35] and may, while agreeing to become a backbencher in Bonn, turn to active vote-getting work at home in Bavaria or Schleswig-Holstein where other qualities count more. It is these members of parliament who are responsible for the public cry for "better," "more specialized," or "trained" representatives. Some critics even demand "exams" for those running for parliamentary elections as well as for those running for public office, forgetting that this would curtail the right of anybody to be elected and finally might shake the foundations of democracy.

At any rate, it is this situation of generalists being confronted with specialized problems which produces results such as those found in an empirical study on the knowledge of financial problems by Bundestag members carried on by Professor Schmölders of Cologne University.[36] He found that knowledge of modern government finance is very limited among members of parliament. This may be the case with many specialized fields. It is not without bitter irony that one notices the method used in conducting empirical studies of this sort. It consists of sampling the opinions of members of parliament to find out their *knowledge* of facts and theories, which can be judged true or false, instead of screening their votes cast after parliamentary debates and judging whether they made good or bad political decisions (which judgment would differ according to the political affiliation of the judge). Political behavior is no longer judged, in accord with democratic doctrine, in terms of whether it is good or bad, but merely by whether it is true or false. It is appraised by "expert knowledge."

However, here we have to quote the remarkable pronouncement of the present Minister of Economics, Schmücker, which he gave as an M.P. in defending his party's platform against Social Democratic experts during the debate on family allowances: "We shall not sacrifice our political will, not even to the arguments of greater expert knowledge" (Wir lassen uns auch nicht durch grösseren Fachverstand von unserer politischen Richtung abbringen).[37] Whether such a phrase represents the expediency of a politician, or whether it is a completely justified attack on something which quite wrongly poses as "objectivity," is open to question. The complexity of the problem is increased when it is the expert, and not the politician, who decides whether objectivity is possible or whether political strength may determine the issue.

Many of the laws in which political strength and expert knowledge are intimately intertwined pass as the work of pure experts. For instance, a law seeming to revise some technical details on stock exchange taxes was passed easily by a majority in the Bundestag; later it turned out to have been designed by the experts of a private banking association to fight a non-associated private stockbroker. The act had to be repealed.[38] Other laws are almost completely written by another group of "experts," the government bureaucracy, which legally is only permitted to give "drafting aid."

It is this mixing up of politics and "Sachlichkeit" (objectivity) which makes the ordinary politician suspicious of the "experts of macroeconomics" who try to convince the politician that the case is already decided by informed thinking. The help of macroeconomic specialists is, so the experts argue, not needed because things have become more complicated and imprecise; on the contrary, many problems which formerly had to be left to majority vote, political combat, or economic competition can nowadays be solved by econometrics. This situation, by the way, is repeated in business management circles when staff people come to feel that their "advice" has, through the perfection of technical methods and tools, turned into a "veto-knowledge" which can be ignored as little as that of engineers in the construction of bridges or houses.

It is clear that both groups—politicians and businessmen— fight to defend themselves against the forceful argument which tries to "think away" their very existence and legitimacy. They fight the same fight against the same opponent, and both their cases can be argued together. Both businessman and politician are, in a market economy and a parliamentary democracy, roles whose actions cannot be predetermined, for whose training there cannot be, in the last instance, objective, teachable, testable criteria. Their way of life is "risk-taking"; their success cannot be, as may be possible with a technician, predetermined if only certain tested rules (of science or experience) are obeyed. Whether a certain action carries success or failure will, in the case of the democratic politician as well as that of the businessman in the market, not be known until afterwards, when and if benefits, profits, votes, victory, and acclamation follow.

The majority of the Bonn Parliament are defending, therefore, not only an economic order that, to the best of their knowledge, opinion, and conviction, has proved its efficiency throughout a decade, but also the very existence and continuance of these two roles. If a rational plan and its execution were to replace economic speculation and political competition and their risks, there might be little scope for them.

This problem is not only a German one, and it will not be pushed to a solution within the scope and lifetime of the Federal Republic alone. But it will be interesting to watch how the younger generation of party leaders and members of parliament who are entering office now and who do not carry the weight of the Weimar ideologies will handle it.

V

Groups and Their Policies

Before describing the policies and behavior of some economic agents, we have to remind the reader that for this part we can only claim very incomplete reporting. It is based on the author's personal experience; some additional research has been done to achieve a somewhat more inclusive picture. Yet with some of the agents reported on, it is merely a listing of suggestions for more intensive research in the future.

BUSINESS ENTERPRISE

Planning in Corporations

Although planning by microeconomic agents does not seem comparable with the economic programing or planning of macroeconomic entities, it is important in a study of national planning to know what entrepreneurs and managers think of planning in their own sphere of action. Experience with microeconomic planning at least increases or awakens an understanding of the possibilities and limits of planning. More important, it indicates the legitimate role that planning can play even in a market system.

In this context it is interesting to note that during the last decade enterprise planning has been spreading in West Germany. It has left the close confines of planned cost control, which had kept it restricted to the accounting department. It has become a matter of concern to top management. The so-called AGPLAN (Arbeitsgemeinschaft Planungsrechnung) in Frankfurt, for example, which brings together business executives, scholars, and consultants to exchange views on planning, has gone far beyond its original purpose of concentrating on accounting.

71

Long-term selling and buying, personnel trends, investment policies, forecasts of market trends, and especially research and development require techniques that depend on plans. A good survey of the state of enterprise planning was made by the Rationalization Congress of the Rationalisierungskuratorium der deutschen Wirtschaft, organized in November, 1962.[1]

It is recognized more and more that planning is not only a process of setting goals for the future and working toward their realization, but that it involves integrating action. A plan requires coordination, the integration of interrelated actions, not simply their intellectual summation. Entrepreneurs, managers, and industrial engineers were familiar with this aspect of the planning process from the organization of production. Here, however, all the factors involved (manpower, machinery, efficiency, time, etc.) were under the control of the planner; they presumably had to obey his commands. With the broadening of the discussion to cover total enterprise planning, including marketing, personnel, investment, and even profit and turnover planning, managers and technicians have become aware of the possibility that a certain type of "planning" is possible even when some factors of a plan are subject to market conditions and are not under complete control of the planner's authority but are the results of a game, gambling, or probability process. This experience with microeconomic planning has helped clear away some of the ideological fog which obscured discussions of macroeconomic planning.

Cooperation among Firms and Branches

Many businessmen—especially from small business—argue that the anticartel laws and the decisions of the Court and Cartel Board regarding it prevent German business from entering into the fruitful cooperation made necessary by the advent of the Common Market.[2] The Anticartel Law explicitly exempts various interfirm combinations, such as rationalization and discount cartels, cartels setting forth specific sales conditions and, to some extent, even specialization cartels. But small business is wary in exploiting these exemptions. In spite of the legal possibilities, they hesitate to cooperate because they are afraid of overstepping the boundaries and incurring the intervention of the Cartel Board.

Nevertheless, there are some forms of inter-firm cooperation.

There may be more than we realize; some are difficult to detect and discuss, since those who engage in cooperative planning are not sure whether or not they are permitted by law to do so. As examples, we might list the agreements by German steel producers on their production programs.[3] Other specialization agreements do not concern production or sales but buying and importing.[4]

It should be noted here that for the coal and steel sector German law has mainly been superseded by the law of the Coal and Steel Community, founded in 1951. The anticartel provisions of the High Authority at Luxembourg differ from the German laws; to some extent, the provisions of the treaty creating the Coal and Steel Community have encouraged certain types of cooperation.[5]

This applies especially to common prognoses of future economic conditions. The German Association of Iron and Steel Industries produces annually a five-year forecast known as the "Aueler Bericht" (named for the castle where the conferees meet). This prognosis is refined and revised each year and comprises forecasts on planned sales of raw and processed steel (domestic and foreign markets are separate), on production capacities and their use and on resource and raw material provisioning (including special transport problems).[6] The same association runs, with the consent of the Luxembourg Authority, a reporting center for all investment plans of the industry. It is open to all concerned and offers information— both global and detailed—on all investment projects.[7] All this prognostic information involves "non-obliging rules" (*unverbindliche Richtgrössen*). Nevertheless, according to one of the top managers of the industry: "Indeed, their influence on enterprise planning seems to be effective enough."[8]

There are other forms of cooperation between firms which transcend branch limits. For instance, automobile and gasoline producers pool their market forecasts in an effort to integrate production plans. It would be interesting to study in detail the branches and sectors of the economy and establish correlations between the proclivity of their managers toward planning, integration, or cooperation, on the one hand, and their market structure and cyclical history on the other.[9]

Fear of collision with the anticartel laws has set up a serious barrier against greater candor in this field of "private macroeconomic programing." At any rate, cooperative planning is an experience through which many firms and branches will go. It will probably contribute toward more understanding by businessmen of the processes of coordination. After all, German business had always been heavily cartelized until 1945, but with the maximization of private profits as a basic purpose. The corporate administration of the Hitler state, in which private business participated, did not change this basic outlook; it only checked it. We think that the present attempts to cooperate will not change the basic outlook either. But at least they will familiarize business with modern methods of cooperation, even if the aim will in some cases remain anachronistic.

Private Banking

German banking, as in any other country, has its own unique structure. This is not the place to explain it in detail. Nor do we wish to argue with those who assert that its characteristic feature consists of its influence on business via stock and bond issues, credit, the votes of those shares which customers have placed into their safes (*depotstimmrecht*), and, finally, interlocking directorates and supervising boards (*Aufsichtsräte*).[10]

Nor do we want to dwell upon another aspect, which seems of some importance to a study of national planning: the concentration process in banking and its effects. So far as this concentration process was a consequence of the typical "division of labor" found in the banking system (the specialization of certain types of banks to certain tasks), it has been attenuated since 1948 by the effects of two currency reforms and the structural changes in capital formation which they caused.[11] Although concentration in certain fields is still impressive, and although government-controlled cartels exist, competition among saving banks and, e.g., giant universal banks—of which there are three in West Germany—is increasing.

In connection with this despecialization, we want to make another observation. By their increasing number and variety of activities, the giant banks gather an amount and a variety of information and influence which could allow for a special sort of programing, coordination, or integration in the corporate sphere. This additional "action parameter" must not necessarily be attributed to a partial control of a market (as with oligopolies). It can simply be the result of the fact that the great size and diversity of financial operations, together with the fact that every business has to deal with a bank because money is the only universal commodity, makes it possible for a giant bank management to counterbalance and— if they carefully integrate all their transactions—to outwit in some respect the Law of Great Numbers, which is the essence of market risk and movement.

One by-product of a large banking business may thus be a lesson in macroeconomic integration and thinking,[12] although the whole business, as a microeconomic entity, still remains a potential victim of incalculable influences from outside. To give a reverse proof: Giant industrial corporations sometimes manage themselves by organizing their central headquarters like a bank, giving or refusing credit and investment facilities to affiliates which are otherwise independent enough to outbid each other or disregard each other's offers (i.e., the Krupp group).

Protected Sectors

As we have seen, the giant banks have moved toward macroeconomic planning entities while remaining in the market and eschewing monopolistic competition. The protected sections of the German economy (e.g., agriculture, potash, coal, housing, milling, etc.) approach the question of programing and planning from just the opposite direction—from outside the market. While a banker and, say, a farmer both tackle substantially the same problem, their attitudes will differ sharply.

The actions of private business groups that are protected and yet integrated into a market economy deserve attention in any study in national economic planning in a democratic society. A distinguishing aspect of a protected industry is usually price control, organized and administered with various degrees of planning, as the enemies of economic planning are always ready to point out. The function and effects of the price control mechanisms vary greatly with each industry. In some, the fixed price is not imposed "from above," but demanded by the organized interests, even if they are the producers and not the consumers of the price-controlled goods. This is very different from the usual type of price control, such as rent control. It is quite natural that tenants should be interested in fixing rents and keeping rent ceilings down, for it is they who would have to pay any increases. In fact, after partial reliberalization of housing, rents have gone up. Minimum prices for food and coal, on the other hand, have been fixed by the producers. In fact, these industries have operated as cartels under state supervision and protection via import restrictions or quotas.

It is the cartel character of these operations which enables us to list their proceedings as actions of private business, although they are more correctly examples of an "administered economy." They are not accompanied by an authoritarian or totalitarian state; they take place within the framework of an ultra-liberalist, parliamentary democracy. The parliament which invented and passed the anticommercial "market regulations" for West German agriculture and the subsidies for coal is one in which, as described above, the legislative process is rooted in the mutual recognition and satisfaction of private interests.

The economic results of these experiences and their relation to planning have been often described as negative. But the political lesson which the technical execution of these protective, antimarket measures may offer remains to be studied. It would be useful to find out, for example, whether these nonmarket measures in a market economy have resulted in breakdown, inefficiency, or black marketeering.

The history of West German coal after 1948 and until the Luxembourg authorities changed the picture remains to be told, and there may be some sad chapters. We cannot do more than raise some questions. The coal industry operated with some degree of autonomy in carrying out the legislation it had asked for. Could it have been more efficient in distributing and allocating its products?[13] If the industry had more readily adapted to consumers' demands, might it still exist quite happily with the noncommercial system which it has had to abandon? Was it *because* it was cartelized that the industry failed to respond to necessity?

The history of West German agriculture is quite different. First, its market regulations were still in full force in 1964. Second, one single administrative measure is sufficient: all domestic production and imported goods have to be channeled through special "Import and Provision Offices" (Einfuhr und Vorratsstellen) which either store them or operate as "sluices" in order to regulate the price. (This system is also used in France and to some extent in the

United States, while Great Britain uses other methods to subsidize her farmers.)

Before ending this discussion, we want to mention briefly a special sort of price control protection based on private agreements: prices to the consumer fixed by the producer and binding on all intermediary distributors. This "Preisbindung der zweiten Hand" (fair trade prices) is allowed by the Anticartel Law for genuine brand name merchandise. Yet it has always been under attack. In many sectors it has quite broken down because of wholesale sales, discount houses, collective buying by workers from firms and offices, and other forms of "gray marketeering."

INTEREST GROUPS AND ASSOCIATIONS

It would by far surpass the scope of this study to describe even briefly the major organizations in the whole range between the individual business firm and official politics and to analyze their behavior in relation to national planning. We will, therefore, limit ourselves to labor unions, management associations, and a general survey of interest associations. The first two are the "partners" in collective bargaining, within the organizational context described earlier. This collective bargaining process and its results represent such an important field for macroeconomic considerations that we shall analyze them separately.

Trade Unions

The orientation of West German trade unions toward national economic planning has been shaped, since 1948, by various factors: their Marxist tradition and its rejection by the majority of voters in the general elections; their conviction, based on their own experience with the National Socialists and their impressions of the Soviet bloc, that planned economies tend to abolish union freedoms; and, finally, the realization that the postwar boom has been achieved by liberalization and competition and against the traditional trade union philosophy.

The result is that, if anyone in the Federal Republic could be called the champion of a mixed economy, it would be the labor unions. The apparently contradictory behavior of the unions in different circumstances can be explained by their eagerness to choose the more "leftist" of alternatives when presented with a specific situation. But very rarely do they offer alternatives themselves.

Hence, the central board of the unions has voted for very rigid, prohibitive anticartel legislation and for a fully independent Central Bank.[14] Even Erhard could not put across these demands, although he also wanted them. On the other hand, unions asked and got co-determination on the firm level in basic industries, and they still want extension of co-determination to all big firms and to the supra-firm level.

The president of the Confederated Unions, Rosenberg, declared in a public statement, in 1964, that "entrepreneurial activity is indispensable."[15] But the program adopted at the Extraordinary Federated Congress, held in November, 1963,[16] had sounded a different note. It called for "macroeconomic frame planning" (*volkswirtschaftlicher Rahmenplan*), nationalization of key industries and other market-dominating enterprises, investment regulations for private business (*Investitionslenkung*), extension of control over public utilities (*Gemeinwirtschaft*) and, most notably, the redistribution of fortunes created in an unjust way.

"Every economy needs planning within a frame of reference which in principle is based on competition" is a union statement which can be listed alongside the Social Democratic statement: "Competition as much as possible, planning as much as necessary."[17] In particular, the unions maintain that the standards of a national budget should be compulsory for government agencies and government-attached boards, and that there should be "orientation data necessary for the proper free decisions within the branches and individual units of the economy." As to investment control, they demand a "selected tax and credit policy including scaled investment allowances" based on "regular published estimates" of demand and need within each single branch. "Thus gross planning by individual private firms could be influenced without depriving each single enterprise of its last and final decision on the kind and size of its investment."

How all this would work has not been put to a test because the political friends of the unions, the Social Democrats, have not come to power in the federal government. SPD-controlled Länder (such as the Land of Hesse, whose constitution was shaped in almost Socialist terms in 1946) cannot change the over-all structure of the economy as long as Bonn is CDU-controlled.[18]

Union action, hence, has had to extend into the areas left free from politics once the major political victory—co-determination in coal and steel—had been won (with help from the Allies, who wanted additional control over the Ruhr "barons"). There is, then, very close cooperation between unions and consumers' cooperatives, including their production units, and between unions and the large building and housing firms owned by them. In this way the German labor union movement, once the ardent champion of nationalization, has built up a major empire of industry, trade, and bank holdings, including a bank chain ranking among the most important credit and investment institutions.

This business empire is run according to traditional business principles, with its cash and capital being used as strike reserves. (Strikes and other forms of collective bargaining will be discussed later.) In general, and with the exception of some unaffiliated unions, the entire union movement has moved toward competition and the market economy. It has, as is commonly said, become "Americanized." At the same time, it has provided programatic justification for the "interventionist" measures which the neoliberalists put into force, albeit with a bad conscience. In this respect, a cynic might say that Professor Erhard, unsystematically and despite himself, executed a policy which later became part of the program of the labor unions.

Management Associations

In November, 1963, the Federation of German Management Associations also published a pamphlet, as a direct challenge to the labor program discussed above.[19] Its first chapter was entitled: "Our political, economic and social order has stood the test." This is quite indicative of the basic attitude of the German employers: they have taken a very strong line on questions of principle. While the pragmatic test may give more weight to the unions' arguments, it has been management which provided the basic philosophy.

With this in mind, it will not be a surprise to learn that management turns down almost every demand of labor that is based on a critique of the existing "order." Hence, extension of co-determination, redistribution of fortunes by central political agencies, and so on have been refused with strong animosity.

In general, management leaders justify this attitude by pointing to the "approved" economic system of neoliberalism and its remarkable success in production and consumption. In particular, it is said that extension of co-determination would lead to an intolerable "concentration of power in the hands of a centrally controlled organizational apparatus," followed by state intervention and destruction of freedom of bargaining. The same holds true for nationalization and investment control. As to macroeconomic forecasting and budgeting, it "could be an important instrument of economic policy," but "it is a task for independent experts."[20]

A contradiction between rigor in principle and leniency in pragmatic situations has marked management policy since the fifties. This contradiction reached a culmination in 1963 in connection with a collective bargaining situation which we shall discuss in the next section. It may prove to have been a turning point in labor-management relations.

Collective Bargaining

Both management and labor agreed in the postwar period that the primary prerequisite of their existence was complete freedom of action without any of the state control practiced under Weimar, Hitler, and the Soviet East.[21] They both welcomed the "de-politization" and reliberalization policy of the Allied and German administrations and the guarantees for freedom of organization written into the federal and several Länder constitutions.[22]

Collective bargaining, consequently, should have developed as a free market activity or, rather, as an expression of monopolized competition, a bilateral monopoly of countervailing powers. The exemption of the labor movement from the anticartel laws, indeed, officially recognized its exceptional role in the market structure.

However, there was, for most of the time, a "limping bilateral monopoly." The index of the real income of the workers illustrates this well.[23] After full employment had been reached (even over-employment, since almost one million foreign workers were imported) scarcity of labor and lack of solidarity on the employers' side gave labor a stronger negotiating position. In the beginning of economic reconstruction, with a labor surplus and scarcity of jobs and of goods in general, the opposite situation had existed. There also might have been, for some time, an inclination on the part of labor to take over-all economic effects into consideration and to be moderate in wage claims.

At any rate, the history of collective bargaining after World War II—which cannot be told here *in extenso*—taught both sides the good and bad consequences of complete freedom of bargaining. This lesson was taught as well to those not involved in bargaining, including pensioners of all sorts, members of the liberal professions, and government officials. Government-insured old age pensions were, in 1957, officially linked to collective bargaining agreements, and participated in wage movements through a social security payment plan tied to wages and productivity.[24] But the rest of the "third force" remained the victims of price increases resulting from collective bargaining agreements.

Public discussion of these collective wage agreements has attracted wide attention to their macroeconomic effects. Each of the "partners" in the bargain naturally tends to impute ill will to the opponent, holding him responsible for any damaging effects a collective contract might have on the economy as a whole. Moreover, each side has its special pleaders who use scientific vocabulary in presenting a host of theorems and formulas to prove and disprove macroeconomic consequences (such as the "productivity formula" to restrain wage increases).[25] The result is a real jungle which, so far, has done more to debunk the prestige of the social scientists involved than to produce a "de-politization" of the issue (*Versachlichung*). This *Versachlichung*—which tentatively may be translated as "the objectivity of expert knowledge" with overtones of impersonality and absence of political trickery—has been given a special department in the Ministry of Labor and Social Order, where methods of drafting collective bargaining agreements are devised. Of course, memories of compulsory arbitration by the state in the Weimar period make it difficult for any government agency to sell such ideas even when they are good. Nevertheless, the law establishing the Expert Council on Economic Development,[26] which officially was prepared in the Ministry of Economics, has a twin born in the Ministry of Labor.

Neither side is too happy about institutionalization of expertise (*Sachverstand*) and *Versachlichung*. Since 1957, a bill has been

introduced, killed, and reintroduced in the federal parliament by
the Liberal party faction which tries to regulate the collective bargaining process as much (and as little) by regular law procedures
as is already done with all civil agreements and contracts, without
the slightest attempt to introduce compulsory arbitration on the
content of these agreements.[27] The bill envisages a sort of legal
channeling, a formalization of the bargaining process, including
strikes and lockouts. Such procedural requirements already exist in
various industries, but were established by collective agreement.
Management agreed to the bill after some hesitation; labor is still
hostile.

Fear of the opponent's, or a neutral expert's, arguments is not
necessarily the determining force in limiting macroeconomic reckoning in wage fights. Each side knows, at heart, that wage fights,
like all commercial negotiations and deals, cannot be "objectively"
(*sachlich*) carried to the point where the loser passes out of economic existence. What is feared is the effect of the opponent's arguments on public opinion, which is difficult to estimate and discount.
In the summer of 1964, both management and labor agreed on a
common evaluation of the price trend in West Germany, both
attributing it to mistakes of government. But they got entangled in
controversy again when they published their common evaluation;
they differed in their analysis of motivations and their interpreta-
tions of the "facts."

Here we are once more confronted with the conflict between
macroeconomic politics and microeconomic psychology. Both sides
have to take into consideration a profit-motivated public; even individual workers do not want to lose their jobs as victims of economic
progress, which they endorse in general. Collective bargaining
always reaches a point where it can be "proved" by either side that
a certain condition (wage level, vacation or sickness pay, or hours
of work) will condemn to economic death this or that particular
agent.

In many branches of industry and trade (even in agriculture)
it is small business which is most directly hit by wage increases.
Mutatis mutandis, this holds true for relations between whole
branches. There are front runners and lame ducks both among individual firms and among economic sectors. The union movement,

organized in a decentralized way but with unified leadership, can always strike at the weakest point, and often does so. Thus the term "to strike at the center of gravity" was coined, applying both to regional and sectoral centers (shop contracts are rarely negotiated in West Germany).

Management, for some time, fell prey to this tactic because it was seriously lacking in solidarity because of the labor scarcity and high liquidity (it was possible to promise and pay higher wages). In 1963, for the first time, such a "gravity strike" was countered by a lockout. It was in a region where big firms would easily have been able to pay what labor wanted. But they chose a lockout to help their colleagues scattered in small—sometimes tiny—businesses all around the region (Baden-Württemberg).

Both strike and lockout lasted for only a brief time before an agreement was reached. Since then "equilibrium" is said to have been restored. But it seems to be an unstable balance. Among younger owner-entrepreneurs and among managers of the "son" generation, especially those who are not production managers with a mass of union-directed workmen, the inclination is growing to settle for some sort of macroeconomic cooperation between labor and management. The lockout has finally made it clear that mere talk of the "partners in the economy" or of the "social partner" (*Sozialpartner*) does not prevent sharp and costly controversies and that accepting the trade unions as "a factor in the political structure" does not settle day-to-day problems.

Experienced managers, as well as entrepreneurs and union leaders, warn against too much optimism and too great expectations from macroeconomic technology. Clear and open bargaining (and that means neoliberalism) prevails on the labor market too. Macro-economic planning techniques are reduced to tactical instruments in this field. In 1960, when Chancellor Adenauer asked the legally independent Central Bank for an expert opinion on what would be tolerable in wage increases in the following year, Bank President Blessing offered a percentage figure. But there was bickering behind the scenes because he had not wanted to be called in as umpire. Although wages were actually raised by much more, the price level remained almost constant. The Presidency of the Central Bank will be reluctant to burn its fingers again by complying with such requests. The president of the Federal Office for Statistics has already turned down a request to preside over an expert committee on wages.[28]

To summarize, management and labor are jealous of safeguarding the "independence" and "autonomy" of their status against all kinds of interventions—political and macroeconomic-technical. At the same time, there is an increasing uneasiness among both "partners" based on the growing conviction that wage agreements of this magnitude and over-all economic importance should not be left only to neoliberalist market tactics. A tendency at least towards longer-lasting agreements is spreading.[29]

Certain actual working mechanisms already indicate that collective bargaining is becoming something more than simple commercial negotiations between bilateral monopolists. For example, contracts signed between the two major organizations are, if requested, declared "binding for all" by the government.[30] Thus, wage or hours regulations negotiated by the executives of a "private group" are made compulsory for any individual whether or not he is a member of that group. This may now have become normal procedure, just as the "closed shop" has become in other countries. Nevertheless, it is as remote from classical economic liberalism as are collectively agreed upon conditions for customers worked out by a group of firms or branch executives and automatically made binding on all customers.

Economic Associations

Some fifty years ago, the legal status of parties was the main concern of political scientists and constitutional jurists. The Bonn Constitution (Basic Law) finally welcomed the political parties within the legal constitutional framework.[31]

But the "Verbände" (pressure groups, economic interest associations, etc.) are still outside the law in the sense that their dominant role in politics and economics is not expressed in what is called in the Roman law tradition "Public Law" (*öffentliches Recht*). They are organized as, and considered to be, private "clubs" or "societies" (*Vereine nach bürgerlichem Recht*), falling under civil law. This applies also to the Bundesverband der deutschen Industrie (BdI), one of the most powerful.[32]

It is interesting to note that this is increasingly resented and that civil law status is no longer considered a sufficient legal classification. After all, these groups *are* "private associations" so long as economic activity is considered to be "private," even when it grows to a size comparable to a small state.

For our study of national planning the arguments pro and con are not as important as the problem of what these associations really are if they can no longer be classified as private *Vereine*. Of first importance is the fact that the big economic associations like BdI do not represent homogeneous interests; they encompass within themselves a great many competing and conflict-ridden smaller groups. From this we can derive one description of their status: they—like the large political parties—are at least required to integrate potential conflict situations within their own ranks.[33] This leads to another demand often made of them: if one of their tasks is the integration of conflicting interests, then they should have well-constructed statutes and procedural regulations so that each member is able to contribute to the formation of the collective will. Sometimes this demand is called the "democratization" of interest groups; at times even a law regulating all this is called for (*Verbändegesetz*). Such demands lead dangerously close to a point where the difference between such organizations and the state has to be made clear.

Second, another point has been explicitly stated in a study on "The Legal Status of Public Groups": "The public groups (*öffentliche Verbände*) do not at all want to appear as moral personalities but as collective organizations. The reason is that they are not very much interested in a formalistic, legal representation of the internal group life against the outer world, e.g. by delegates. They are mainly interested in demonstratively representing all their members in public."[34]

Here we touch upon the most crucial point of the entire issue. When an economic association—such as the BdI—can no longer be regarded as a group of persons organized for a special purpose (for instance, rabbit breeding or stamp collecting) but has to be viewed as a group formed for demonstrating and representing its members in public, then what, actually, is it that is being demonstrated or represented? And in what respect does such an organization differ from a political party organized as a "special interest party," such as the refugee party?

The associations themselves assert that they do not represent a political interest, but "their declared aim is the transformation of private interests of many individuals into a common public interest, the authentic representation and demonstration of the group's interest as the interest of the whole."[35] Even when, in terminating a conflict between two organizations, each of them has to sacrifice something of its former objectives in what is usually called a compromise, this compromise is sold to the public, and the public is called upon to support it, as if it were not a temporary, provisional agreement (which used to be the meaning of compromise), but "a status-giving contract (*Statusvertrag*) within the frame of an order which fictitiously claims to be free of conflict." The author just quoted calls that "wrapping a compromise into ideology."[36]

The problem is as yet unsolved. Are we witnessing, here, a revival of a sort of corporate state in which groups whose inner motive remains profit seeking cloak themselves in a fictitious interest of the whole? Or are we seeing the emergence of something new where the very existence of economic activity—apart from its profit-making—becomes a political issue which justifies agitation?[37]

We think that it is not a question of one or the other, but both. If, however, the existence of limited economic groups can be justified from the standpoint of the political whole, then it must also be legitimate to study them from the standpoint of macroeconomics. Such a legitimation can no longer be countered by simple commercial arguments. If an economic group claims a political right to keep the members of the group (or the entire group as such) from going bankrupt, they have to present a justifying criterion for their existence other than profitable production or consumption.

It is here that we find an important open issue on social development, one which makes the problem of economic associations a test of West Germany's attitude toward national planning. Again, the problem is intimately tied to what can be made "objective" and what cannot. The BdI sponsors, in joint cooperation with the Management Association, one of the economic research institutes discussed in the next chapter, the Deutsche Industrieinstitut. Yet its scientific status is open to question. When Erhard publicly criticized the industrial morale of German labor, he had to listen to the reply of a labor leader who said: "Do you know that you repeat,

by saying this, the biased (*unsachliche*) propaganda of the Industrieinstitut?"[38]

INSTITUTIONS OUTSIDE GOVERNMENT

The Role of Universities and Professors

This study of national planning touches only upon the politico-
economic role of university and professorial research, study, and
teaching: it is not concerned with the academic world as a whole.

Debates on planning, as on the economic system in general, are
the academic property of the economists. A sharply drawn, and
jealously maintained, line between the faculties causes an academic division of labor which does not contribute to clearer understanding. University reform designed to overcome this obstacle is
lamentably slow moving.[39] Since the economics chairs are set up by
"schools" (neoliberalists, post-Keynesians, moderate social-demo-
crats, etc.), it is difficult for laymen—hence for politicians and the
general public—to judge the degree of bias inherent in an expert's
opinion.

Since World War II the political entanglement of the West German professor of social science (i.e., his entanglement in politics,
mostly in the guise of an adviser or expert consultant) has consider-
ably increased. Several professors have achieved cabinet rank.

For the layman this further increases the professor's prestige,
which already—according to public opinion polls—tops all other
professions. For the initiated, it has not always tended to enhance
esteem for the "science" represented by the "political" professor. In
general, it can be said that the prestige of the natural scientist (such
as medicine, physics, chemistry, all applied technical disciplines)
ranks, at present, far above that of the social scientist and the
humanities scholar. Perhaps this is a result of the political events
of the first half of this century.

However, all this applies more to the opinion of the public than
to the judgment of those responsible leaders who ask for professorial advice. Here the advice is classified according to its usefulness,
i.e., how much it serves the purposes and desires of those who seek
the advice and who will be in more cases than not a special interest
group. Here again, suspicion is aroused among the sophisticated

that a professor heavily engaged in politics or political economics may become a special pleader. "Neutral," "value-free" science, as it was once demanded by Max Weber, is explicitly rejected by some scholars as not only sterile but unattainable.[40]

Extra-University Research Institutes

There are a number of noncommercial, non-university economic research institutes which must be considered in a discussion of the role of macroeconomic thinking and planning in West Germany. They are mostly concerned with economic trends and forecasts, either for the whole economy or for individual areas. Sometimes they are the successors of former research institutes on business cycles, such as the Deutsche Institut für Wirtschafts-forschung, Berlin-Dahlem, formerly Institut für Konjunkturfor-schung, founded in 1925 by Professor Wagemann, then president of the Reich Office for Statistics. Others belonging to this category are the IFO Institut für Wirtschaftsforschung, Munich, the Welt-wirtschaftsinstitut, Hamburg, and the Wirtschaftswissenschaftliches Institut der Gewerkschaften (WWI).

The institutes are grouped together in a "Arbeitsgemeinschaft deutscher wirtschaftswissenschaftlicher Forschungsinstitute e.V." which emphasizes its scientific independence. It is interesting to note that the Wirtschaftswissenschaftliche Institut (WWI), financed by the Federal Organization of the Trade Unions, is enrolled as a member of this organization but that the Institute run under the joint direction of the Federation of German Industries and of the German Management Associations (Deutsches Industrieinstitut) is not.

Most of the institutes are based on statutes which try to guarantee their independence and regulate the type of research they may engage in, or the kind of commissions they are allowed to accept. Financing is provided for in various ways. The Berlin Institute, for example, is supported by a board of trustees representing various ministries of the federal government, the Berlin Senate, several Länder of the Federal Union, banking, trade and industry, parties, labor unions, and a specially created "Union of Friends of the Institute."

The institutes cooperate in various ways with many government and semigovernmental activities, as well as with private groups. Some of them are, for instance, members of a group created by the

Federal Ministry of Finance for pre-estimating tax revenues, an important activity for determining the scope of the budget each year in a country in which the Constitution prohibits deficits,[41] but equally important as an exercise in macroeconomic forecasting, indispensable even in a market economy.

All these institutes publish reports and forecasts of the economy's development at regular intervals, mostly annually. Usually these reports differ in color, sentiment, and mood. The differences can, by the initiated, be correlated with an institute's administrative presidents or its sponsors, but no hint of undue influence will necessarily be implied. The reports of *Konjunktur* of all the institutes together constitute something like an open debate on which others may base their own judgments. It has happened that all the published forecasts will be proved wrong subsequently by later events.

Knowledge of the different forecasts and macroeconomic judgments helps in applying relative values to allegedly scientific data. But the situation becomes even more perplexing when a new source of conflict is added to the chorus of economic observers from the different ministries of the federal government and Länder. There have been instances in which a federal minister himself has reduced over-all economic growth estimates elaborated by the joint action of several institutes and ministries. Because he wanted to influence labor's wage claims, the minister deemed such manipulation necessary before publishing the figure.

This is another demonstration that macroeconomic reasoning within the context of a market society is unavoidably condemned to become, itself, a commercial service. It ranks with all kinds of tactical or strategic psychological influences emanating from profiteering and speculative agents in the economy. The institutes described above seem to be aware of this situation. There is need for further study of how the "suprapartisan credibility" sought in macroeconomic planning can be attained in an environment of competitive economic analysis.

Marketing Consultants and Opinion Polls

There is, naturally, a host of "service" businesses of this type, either independent, linked to a business cycle research institute, or part of a broader commercial service, such as designing, advertising, or marketing in general. Some of these institutes—for which

"Infratest GmbH" in Munich may stand as a good example—go very far toward macroeconomic thinking when establishing and justifying their advice, e.g., when evaluating specific consumption or investment behavior and their long-term changes. The same is true of public opinion polls which are made to order.

Here again, in our judgment, it is the educational result rather than the strict dependence on figures which counts: management and the public are made familiar not only with the existence of, but with the necessity for, prognostic activities, with their methods, scope and limits, and with their place within a commercial system. At present the use of prognostic instruments, based on knowledge and reckoning rather than on rule of thumb and speculation, seems to be preferred by large corporations, whereas small business and its entrepreneurs (often described as very conservative) seem to mistrust consultant firms and, especially, marketing consultants.

Among forecasting experts, there seems to be unanimous agreement that macroeconomic reasoning is based, technicalities aside, on four sets of convictions and assumptions:

(1) that the economic structure, as a mathematical-logical system, can be ascertained, understood, and made transparent (e.g., by input-output studies, etc.);

(2) that over-all economic growth "occurs" harmoniously and within certain limits, or is kept so circumscribed by external interventions (political stability);

(3) that consumption (and saving) behavior "occurs" along a certain predictable path, e.g., following the over-all way set by the technically more advanced countries (including technical progress through inventions);

(4) that the "countervailing powers" operating in the country, as well as those influencing it from abroad (big business, finance, labor, etc.), are themselves interested in stability and help maintain it.

To these factors must be added a fifth which applies to all kinds of macroeconomic reckoning, i.e., to all items dealt with in this whole study. It is of ultmost importance to know the way the original data, from which all the macroeconomic technique starts, are provided and the degree of their precision. Here we merely touch upon a critical problem which we shall take up again in the next section.

A final word on the macroeconomic function of consulting services: a noncommercial institute, usually serving at least an entire sector, will make a forecast (say, shrinking market) and may perhaps add, as a consequence, a warning to go slow in production. But the consultant to a single firm may use a forecast competitively and advise: "Let us enlarge our share in the shrinking market and increase production." Here there are sharp differences between two approaches to macroeconomic thought and action.[42]

INDEPENDENT GOVERNMENT INSTITUTIONS

Enterprises and Public Utilities

Strictly speaking, enterprises owned and operated by public authorities do not always belong to the category of "independent government agencies." This term should be applied only to those which carry out public tasks in a noncommercial way, *"Anstalten"* (institutions), boards, and, in some instances, *"Regiebetriebe"* or *"Versorgungsbetriebe"* (public utilities). In contrast, profit-seeking enterprises which are government owned only "by chance," and which could be run by private owners just as well, cannot be termed government agents in the same sense.

However, we still want to list under this heading all kinds of economic units operating under public influence, in a commercial or noncommercial way, with "public" all levels of state and government administration: Federal, Länder, county, municipality, or other. Clear-cut divisions are difficult in this field and in a country where age-old public monopolies compete with the most modern forms of government intervention. The type of government activity described as *"Staatswirtschaft," "Staatskapitalismus,"* or *"Gemeinwirtschaft"* has grown in West Germany to such a huge complexity that at this point nothing more can be done than just to list some of the major ones and their planning implications. We shall proceed from the merely formal to those with the most substantial government influence.

First, there are the purely commercially motivated enterprises which for historical reasons, or by pure chance, are owned by governmental authorities, or rather, in the tradition of continental law, not by individual authorities, but by the "fisc" (a fictitious entity created in monarchist times to separate public property from the court treasury). Here again we have to separate the ownership of enterprises which operate in a competitive market from the owner-ship of monopolies, either "natural" or "artificial" (such as the match and alcohol monopolies, created by law in Germany).

Ownership of competitive enterprises includes:

(1) Volkswagenwerk, the biggest West German enterprise (and twenty-ninth on the world list)—partially returned to private ownership in 1960;

(2) approximately 70 per cent of the aluminum industry;

(3) stock shares in some other industries, up to 70 per cent, among them mining, steel, non-ferrous metals, shipbuilding, oil refining, chemicals, and recently, movie production;

(4) the huge chain of the municipality-owned (and tax-privileged) savings banks;

(5) the state-owned commercial and mortgage banks; be-tween 50 and 70 per cent of the banks of this type are govern-ment owned;

(6) the state share in the whole credit business increased from 49 per cent in 1950 to 55 per cent in 1960;

(7) special state-owned banks for economic development, such as Kreditanstalt für Wiederaufbau;[43]

(8) housing construction;

(9) 90 per cent of all producers of electricity, who increased their controlling share of total production from 74 per cent in 1950 to 85 per cent in 1960.[44]

The neoliberalists have been attacking this huge embodiment of state capitalism as being theoretically avoidable.[45] A bill was intro-duced in the Federal Parliament under which some important re-privatizations, such as Preussag and Volkswagenwerk, have taken place. Yet denationalization procedures have not always proceeded very strictly along commercial lines; Volkswagen shares, for exam-ple, were "sold" with social discounts. The state's share after re-privatization of the corporation has not been reduced to zero.[46]

There has been little evidence that government has tried to make use of its holdings in any way much different from what a market controlling trust in private hands would do. Social Democrats, who have always wanted to push government ownership toward *Gemeinwirtschaft,* have complained often about the many lost opportunities and have naturally opposed re-privatization. The Federal Union and the Länder controlled a large group of Volkswagen shares when Erhard resorted to threats of tariff reduction, trying to prevent a Volkswagen price rise.[47]

The situation in government-owned (sometimes government-created) monopolies is peculiar to Germany and distinctly different from many other countries. Here ownership reaches from railroads (all except very small ones) to the telegraph and telephone, radio broadcasting and television, to many municipal public utilities, including transport systems. Enterprises of this sort have been regarded since time immemorial as the domain of public administration; the public is used to "obeying" the railroad conductor. Selling a ticket is, legally, an act of authority, not a business. There are signs, at present, that some of these monopolies are becoming imbued with a more commercial spirit (e.g., the advertisement and price campaign of the railroads, which encounter competition from automobiles, trucks, buses, ships, and air traffic). But most of the behavior of public monopolies remains very close to that of public administration and, in this respect, cannot be treated separately from truly noncommercial economic government activities, such as the postal service.

There have been attempts—especially in social-democratic Länder and town administrations—to integrate all public enterprises and institutions into one *Gemeinwirtschaft* concept. There are similar attempts on an international scale, such as those of the "collective economy" started by Edgar Milhaud.[48] As for the Federal Republic, there seems to be little evidence of any systematic integration of government-owned enterprises and public utilities. They are scattered among many hands, which are either out of touch with each other because of geographic separation or compete with each other (e.g., for labor, energy, and capital). Generally, one could say that it is the market which has, in the last instance, integrated even the economic activities of the government. It may be interesting to note in this context that "public authorities" such as counties, towns, municipalities, villages, etc., join together in organizations of private character to form pressure groups to influence legislation just as industry, labor, and farmers do. An example is the Deutsche Städtebund—Federation of German Cities.

Central Bank

The Central Bank (Deutsche Bundesbank, formerly Bank Deutscher Länder, formerly Reichsbank) has a rich history. What interests us here is the role of this institution in present-day macroeconomic issues. First, we have to state as emphatically as possible that a Central Bank, as an agency with a monopoly on the issuing of paper money, may continue to behave, even when the gold standard has been legally or *de facto* abandoned, as a bank in the full commercial sense; giving and refusing credit, and buying and selling foreign exchange, metals, and commercial paper.[49]

This is the case so long as those authorities entitled to control the actions of the Central Bank (owners, even government owners, boards, ministries) permit commercial behavior by the bank. This does not necessarily mean profit-seeking behavior, but at least the kind of safeguarding of the commercial liquidity represented by the kind of money which the Central Bank itself cannot create. Regularly this will be foreign exchange and foreign holdings. In other words, the Central Bank remains a bank in the full sense so long as it is fully integrated into a free international money market with its many ramifications.

If a Central Bank is given—and guaranteed—this character, it is the direct opponent of any planned macroeconomic system for systematic-logical reasons rather than because of any psychological motivations of its managers. In West Germany the Central Bank has from its re-creation by Allied authorities (prior to the re-creation of a German central political administration) until today, legally enjoyed complete independence from state interference in its bank transactions.

However, political independence was not guaranteed as far as the targets of these bank transactions are concerned. There the Central Bank is, on the contrary, operating under legal rules unknown to simple commercial banks. Consequently, the Bank has *de facto* developed into a kind of macroeconomic super-institution which nevertheless tries to execute its tasks via the credit system, thereby seeking to maintain a money-operated market economy.[50] It is the Central Bank which, in West Germany as elsewhere, is by law held partially responsible (for good reason or not) for the economy's achieving such macroeconomic goals as price stability, exchange stability, and full employment.[51] These are tasks which presuppose a post-liberalist monetary system; in times of gold currency it would have been impossible to credit a Central Bank with attaining such targets.

When analyzed systematically, macroeconomic targets of this sort turn out to be "plans" and not "universal laws" in the legal sense. The West German Central Bank, though legally kept completely free and independent has, therefore, not been able to escape thinking, even acting, along noncommercial lines and in several instances has come into severe conflict with other "planning" and "plan-executing" agencies. For example, the Bundesbank had to follow suit in 1961 when the Cabinet (led by the Minister of Economics for economic reasons and by the Chancellor for political reasons) ordered re-evaluation of the German currency, although some Bank presidents were against the monetary change. Again, in 1956, there was an open clash between the Bank management, which had just restricted credit in order to control a boom (an action which displeased industry), and the Chancellor who, on the occasion of the Annual Convention of German Industry, aligned himself with the industrialists.[52] The Bank has in more cases than one, by autonomous action of its board, restricted free international money flows in order to ban "hot" money, which was allegedly causing inflation, from entering the country, or has made its entry more difficult or uninteresting by cutting interest or discount rates for foreign money deposits.

These examples show that sharing responsibility for the attainment of macroeconomic goals may destroy the banking character of the Central Bank. This has happened in West Germany. Nevertheless, the classical view of a Central Bank as a banking institute is still acclaimed by the public, the law, the legislature, government, and the bank boards themselves in West Germany. Memories of two inflations caused by state intervention inhibit public reflection—and action—on the problem of what the Central Bank actually has become and how it should be re-integrated into the macroeconomic process. What is acknowledged by all is that the government cannot derive any rights from the formal legal fact of holding the Bank's capital. Moreover, the Bank has been delegated a task besides sell-

ing, buying, and controlling the money market and giving or refusing credit: observing the economy as a whole and reporting
thereon. The Annual Reports, and the *Bundesbankbericht,* published monthly, are two of the Central Bank publications which are
without reservation ranked among the best of their sort by central
banking colleagues in other industrial countries. They have long
since ceased to be reports on the Bank's commercial situation and
have become concerned with macroeconomic statistics, judgments,
and forecasts.

Statistical Bureaus

The Central Bank's economic department would have already
become a kind of Statistical Bureau of the Federal Union were it
not for the existence of an independent institution on the federal
level corresponding to similar agencies on a regional level. The
Statistiche Bundesamt and the Landesämter attached to the Länder
have a reputation for serving statistical purposes of many kinds. A
special law passed in 1953 reformulated these tasks and especially
the authority of the Federal Office to gather economic data from
private agencies.[53]   On the occasion of the introduction and discussion of this bill there were controversies once again on the scope
of macroeconomic statistics, notably on the problem of whether
traditional national budgeting (volkswirtschaftliche Gesamtrech-
nung) should be extended to encompass macroeconomic *ex ante*
budgeting and what the role of the Bundesamt would be in that
case.

The 1953 law provided the first integrated regulation of the
organization and legal basis of data-gathering procedures and
processing in Gemany. To the Federal Office is attached a Beirat
(Council of Advisors) whose members are representatives of
federal ministries, of the Federal Budget Controller's Court
(Bundesrechnungshof), the Central Bank, the Federal Railway, the
Central Associations of the Municipalities, of industry and other
business, of labor and of the economic research institutes.

The Federal Statistical Bureau gathers and processes data; it
has no role or authority in forecasting or planning. Its president
once turned down a request to head a "neutral experts' board"
which was "to control [in the sense of observation and evaluation
capital. Moreover, the Bank has been delegated a task besides sell-

this would have been "a political task, whereas the public expects from the head of the Federal Statistical Bureau objective data."[54]

Again we run into the controversy between political and scientific motivations. The refusal of the president of the Statistical Bureau intimates that objective, nonpolitical control, observation, and evaluation of past events is possible in a market economy. The fact that even the mere reported data of the past are very often the source of a political controversy shows that "objectivity" in this context is double-faced: whether past data are correctly reported is, in a market economy torn by conflicting interests, very often a matter not only of exact observation and good reckoning but also of rival theories, and sometimes even of plans for the future made by the divergent groups.

The Federal Bureau of Statistics has so far managed to keep itself free of the most controversial issues. Yet the Federal Bureau of Statistics has been made the permanent secretarial office of the newly established expert council on economic issues. Whether it will continue to present itself as a kind of "general secretary" for data or will be thrown into the troubles of a pluralistic society may soon become clear.

Social Security

National economic planning and social security are closely connected in various ways. First, social insurance in its very essence is an attempt to organize counter-instruments against an unplanned market society. This holds true even in those cases where social security is designed to resemble commercial insurance operations as closely as possible. The law of great numbers on which these techniques are based may be destroyed in times of economic crisis. German unemployment "insurance" was floored by the drain on insurance reserves in 1930. Even without such a crisis, no social security instrument can exist in West Germany without government subsidies.

These subsidies provide a second link between social security and planning. To estimate future budget charges, the government has to gather prognoses on macroeconomic data, such as demographic development, age of population, structure of the economy, etc. In West Germany, consolidated social security costs have risen from 11.7 billion Deutsche Mark in 1950 to 55.3 billion (estimated) in 1964. This means a rate of increase of 400 per cent during a period in which the GNP rose by 300 per cent.[55] Macroeconomic reckoning has been very much complicated by the introduction in 1957 of the "dynamic scheme" linking the rate of pensions to the index of wages and productivity.[56] The new law prescribes the regular calculation and publication of the "balance prognoses based on insurance calculation techniques" (*versicherungstechnische Bilanzen*) covering all social security institutions for the next thirty years. This means forecasting the receipts, expenses, and capital stock of those institutions in which the major parts of the economic money flow are concentrated.

This leads to a third link between planning and social security: the social security institutions are important money-lending centers which come close to influencing capital and other markets, such as housing and construction. Centralized influence on their lending behavior is, in spite of substantial subsidies, weak in West Germany. Sometimes they are attacked for having added to the "build-up" of a boom.

Most important in the Federal Republic are—to list a few—workers' health insurance, workers' invalid and old age insurance, unemployment insurance linked with a National Employment Office organization, employees' old age insurance (separate from workers', with different conditions), miners' insurance (traditionally separate), and accident insurance. All of these are compulsory, with employers paying all (as in accident insurance) or half of the contributions not taken over by the state. Compulsory employees' insurance reaches only to a certain maximum income (1964, 1,250 DM monthly); there are other limits for health insurance. But less than 5 per cent of the total labor force is excluded by these limits, and the excluded area is reduced steadily.

The monopoly-like grip of some of these compulsory insurance organizations is considerable, not only on private insurance companies (life, health), but also in other respects. For instance, employment office activity is by law restricted to the official employment organization; private agencies are forbidden by law. A court judgment on this point is based on almost medieval thinking.[57]

The entire social security system was elevated to a completely different status when the tie to the wage and productivity index was enacted in 1957. For every newly granted pension an index formula is set up which automatically links the pension to a complicated mixture of the wage productivity movement of recent years. For the already existing pensions, this link can be established by a vote of the federal Parliament on the recommendation of the Council of Social Advisers (Sozialbeirat) which was established by this law. The Council has always recommended a substantial rise, and Parliament has passed it. The experts have had a hard job—as have those who staffed the Council, because they had to take into consideration the "affiliations" of the allegedly "neutral" experts. The Council once broke up on a hot problem of macroeconomics and had to be reconstituted.

Economic Advisers and Expert Councils

Many important federal ministries have attached to themselves permanent councils of scientific experts. In most cases the members are economists; in almost all cases they are full professors. To them must be added the Sozialbeirat and the Sachverständigenrat (expert council) created by special law in 1963 and attached to the government's executive branch in general, not to a special ministry.[58] The expert councils submit "opinions" (Gutachten) at regular intervals or *ad hoc*. The publication of these opinions is sometimes withheld; sometimes (as in the case of the expert council created by law in 1963) publication of regular opinions is mandatory. In either case, the decision is considered a matter of high policy. For instance, the expert group attached to the Ministry of Economics had, for some time prior to 1961, recommended re-evaluation of the currency to counter imported inflation. Their opinion was not published until 1961 when re-evaluation took place.

Another expert opinion has been worked out on the problem of long- and middle-term budget planning (four to six years) at the federal level. The advisers want budgetary planning restricted to informative forecasting and to data concerning the economy as a whole, plus a few compact blocs such as foreign aid, social security, road building, defense, and housing construction. They warn against any attempts to make forecasting the basis of control "by any means," and against any far-reaching subdivision of the data, "or else the market economy would be in danger."[59]

The staffing requirements of the newly created General Expert Council may be taken as indicative of the functions and problems of these groups. The law closely controls selection of members. The five Expert Council members who were finally called in 1964 by the federal president (a procedure resembling the appointment of a minister) are three professors (two teaching at universities, one heading an independent economic research institute), one former Land minister attached to the Social Democrats, now "labor director" of a co-determined industrial plant, and one former Secretary of State attached to the Christian Democrats, formerly director of a banking institute, now business adviser and member of various boards of supervisors (Aufsichtsrat).

Such a composition intimates that a double task is called for: the members should be independent experts, and at the same time command the good will of the major political and economic groups (political parties, business, and labor) by a sort of proportional representation principle. Perhaps a third quality was sought: they should possess high public status. At any rate, it was hoped that they would, as a collective body, try to perform the task of a good member of Parliament (no longer always realized): namely, represent the whole of the people. But they have not been given appropriate authority to attempt that, although the law does allow for the publication of dissenting opinions.

Their dilemma showed clearly when, in 1965, they came out with their first regular expert report on economic trends. They proposed flexible exchange rates to stop "imported inflation." The government, headed by the Chancellor himself, all the political parties, and a vast majority of all interest groups spoke up against the "experts," referring to them as "entirely theoretical," "professors," "unpolitical," etc. Thus, their much-cherished "neutral" authority was dragged into high politics on the very first occasion— while at the same time they were reproached for unpolitical behavior.

Here again the political and administrative structure has not yet overcome a difficulty which has plagued politics and economics since the division of labor broke up the self-sufficient household: to maintain a clear-cut division between politics, economics, and technical expertise.

There seems to be a new method of looking for a solution to this dilemma, that of setting up new "expert" circles whose proper role in politics cannot as yet be determined. Some forty years ago the fashionable answer to the problem was the establishment of a "third chamber" in parliament to represent economic and social interests, the Reichswirtschaftsrat (Reich Economic Council). France still has such an institution. In West Germany the demand to reconstitute this Weimar institution can sometimes still be heard; its nuclei are either sought or found in the organizations of the Chambers (of Commerce, Agriculture, Trade, Artisans, etc., to which should be added a Chamber of Labor)[60] or in the organizations of the "social partners"—management and labor. The latest example of this political demand comes from the president of the German Employees' Union (Deutsche Angestelltengewerkschaft), who publicly called for a Federal Economic Council composed of "Social partners and independent economists" which could function as a "deliberating body taking precedence over Parliament." He maintained that the work of an expert council deprived of any authority would be nothing but a "playful platonic exercise."[61]

FORMAL GOVERNMENT AGENCIES

Parties and Parliaments

Parties here are considered as formal governmental agencies since they are (for the first time in German history) explicitly mentioned in the federal constitution of 1949.[62] Furthermore they are beginning—as are the economic associations—to fulfill the same type of important integrating function, both economically and socially, as would be expected of a plan. It is the same integrating function of the West German parliaments, rather than their legislative, budgeting, or control functions, that is under discussion here.

Hence, parties and parliaments are spoken of as arenas for economic deliberation, exchange, interchange, and integration. Earlier it was noted that modern parliaments (and hence political parties) are becoming more and more like markets. We have said that a member of parliament (of parties, too) very often does not act as a representative of the whole in the Burkian sense but as the delegate of an interest group.[63] This is underlined by the fact that parties (as well as parliaments) more or less provide for proportional representation of interests and their organized groups. In West Germany this holds true almost as much for the part of parliament, which is elected by direct vote, where one man carries the district by a majority of the votes, as for the other half, which is elected by proportional representation among the parties.

What is more important, this tends to hold true more and more for both large parties (CDU/CSU and SPD) and to a lesser extent for the smaller Liberalists (FDP). It did not apply at all, of course, to special interest parties such as the BHE (Refugees' party) which are no longer present in the Federal Parliament.

Election trends seem to show that the "integrative" party, which encompasses and represents many interests, will be the future political organization or, at least, the future party campaign machine. This shows that the parties and parliaments are already in the process of becoming what is sought from another direction, "economic councils."

Proper procedures for accommodation within parties, however, are still lacking. The devices in practice, such as bargaining for votes with veto groups or mixed-package legislation, are makeshift. The leading circles of a party (as of a parliament) will eventually have to turn to other methods for winning the support of heterogeneous interest factions. The most logical one will be to present policy and legislation programs, not as a host of immediate proposals but as step-by-step propositions ordered in a sequence. Some politicians have unsuccessfully tried to do this.[64] They may be more effective once they have proved that they can "keep the plan" just as one "keeps a promise," because special interest groups will then feel more sure that their demands will be met if they wait until the date of planned performance.

Thus the very first steps are being taken in the direction of making parties (and parliaments) anticipate the tasks which they still try to delegate officially to the executive branch and advisory experts, but which are essentially political in nature and therefore belong to those agents who shape and formulate the political will: the integration of economic interests through a sequence of activities over time, in other words, planning.

Government Budgets

To what extent does monetary federal budgeting involve any national programing or planning functions?

Certainly in order to make an estimate of the income side of the budget, forecasting is needed; there is an advisory council which helps the Minister of Finance do just that. Incidentally, the Ministry of Finance, for a long time, collected secret information, available only from tax collection records, on which it based its forecasts but which was also of great importance for any national accounting on the structure of the income pyramid formed by taxpayers. The first Minister of Finance, by steadily underestimating the tax income and lagging behind in defense expenses, amassed a reserve of up to eight billion marks at the Central Bank, a sort of "anticyclical monetary policy achieved by chance." This reserve was heavily attacked and finally spent—"three times" over, as some critics say. It aroused the desire for money on the part of domestic and foreign politicians, and at the end the Defense Ministry presented its postponed budget bills.

Public debate on the programed expenditures in the federal budget—as against receipts—has been very animated. One might think that a budget which seems to be the chance result of conflicting interests and which does not extend its scope for more than one year must have very little meaning in terms of national planning. However, two points are being made to refute this.

First, it is said that the very size of the federal budget (in 1963, 56.9 billion marks of a GNP calculated as 376 billion marks)[65] influences economic growth (expressed in money units) even when the expenditures are scattered over many sections of the economy and even when the entire budget is covered by ordinary receipts. Huge increases in government expenditures, when planned, published, and executed through the budget, are said to have a self-fulfilling effect by producing just enough tax receipts as are needed to cover the expenditures. Their psychological effect is said to be sufficient to achieve this. A cumulative income tax system, in connection with this psychological effect, is held responsible for the fact that the government share of the GNP has grown more rapidly than the GNP in recent years.[66] Generally, it is said that the federal budget produces an inflationary trend even when balanced in any sense.

Second, a programing effect is produced by the "frozen" parts of the budget expenditures, which are said to amount to more than 80 per cent.[67] This again is used as a justification of the need for more government planning. Economists, trade unions, and Social Democrats argue that compulsory business bookkeeping should be introduced, forcing the state to make book entries for long-term debts and commitments.[68] Many experts advocate four to six year budgetary periods. The system would be similar to individual firm budgeting: one year in detail and the following four or five years sketched in broad programs, thus allowing for flexibility.

In this connection questions of control have often come up. How can any person or any group not working in the statistical or executive bureaucracies exert any sensible degree of control over the accuracy of the figures in the huge volume of the annual budget? Opposition members in the Bundestag have attacked the Minister of Finance for "making up" figures for the budget.[69] It is on this point, the empirical problem of collecting reliable data, that the most pragmatic opponents of any extension of planning may, in the future, attack its present champions.

We skip, for the sake of brevity, a discussion of the planning effect of the many individual taxes known in West Germany. We merely mention in passing that the "Galbraith criticism" has in the meantime also reached Germany, i.e., that interventions should be planned to divert purchasing power from the "socially unnecessary, exuberantly and, in an anarchic way, growing luxurious private consumption to the socially indispensable orderly consumption of state welfare."[70] Erhard presented, in 1965, the vague idea of a giant special fund to cope with this problem, ("Gemeinschafts-werk," a sort of "forced community chest"). The fund (1 per cent of GNP) should be protected from ordinary budgeting pro-cedure and run by "experts" in order to prevent ordinary M.P.'s from spending it for subsidies or vote-getting purposes. Finally, it is interesting to note that German administrative law has long used the term "plan" to describe the budget, which is still called a *"Haushaltsplan"* (household plan of government). Positions for personnel inscribed in the budget are called *"Planstellen,"* which translated means "to be on the payroll."

Executive Plans Outside the Budget

A series of long- and medium-term measures taken by the fed-eral government and explicitly labeled "plans" needs special atten-tion. These measures represent an attempt to establish and reach targets for economic policy within special sectors. Among these are the "Green Plan" of farm subsidies, the "Bundesjugendplan" (Fed-eral Youth Plan), a Road Construction Plan (Verkehrsplan), and

"Raumplan" (Spatial Plan) which is, for public relations reasons, called "Raumordnung."

First, we want to make it clear that we do not consider that everything which bears the label "plan" is one in the sense of being a timetable of prescribed actions whose working out by the joint efforts of a large group will produce some desired effects. The plans just mentioned are all of a quite different order. Some of them are simply ideas of what one could do without any legislative standing in a legal sense, or any executive setup in a "planning" sense.

The Youth Plan is a plan with some executive structure, although it has little logical coherence. Under the plan, subsidies to youth organizations are based on criteria which have been fixed once and for all, so that the plan is really a law in the juridico-logical sense.[71] In a much less precise sense, one has become accustomed to speak of a "Golden Plan" for sport and recreation facilities and a "White Plan" for the construction of hospitals and the planned education of physicians. Both these plans lack precision as well as administrative stringency. The Road Construction Plan is a nonbinding program of the Ministry of Transport.

Finally, the "Green Plan" comprises an integrated description of an economic sector exempted from the market. All agricultural subsidies, in figures, are listed according to their purpose, and the plan has a binding legislative and executive effect. Interestingly enough, one speaks of the "Green Plan" both in the singular and in the plural. Officially, a Green Plan is the annual agricultural subsidy budget based on the annual Green Report (Grüner Bericht), which again is based on the law regulating the annual subsidies.[72]

Ostensibly, this law was meant to help West German agriculture adapt to new situations and circumstances which had developed because of political events (such as the loss of the agrarian territories in the East) or technological change (such as industrialization of other countries' agriculture). Basically, it was designed as a transitional measure to help German peasants to become farmers.

Were it not for the fact that the annual Green Plans are made up in figures and for the fact that the annual Green Report presents consolidated farm balances and incomes, the Green Plan would be simply a policy. It is, in our judgment, the mathematical techniques which enable control of this highly political activity. For instance, starting with the Green Plan of 1964, the table of data has been broken up into three (instead of the former two) categories of "help": first, subsidies given to ameliorate the effects of agricultural structure (such as the scattered location of farm lands) and low working and living conditions in the country (including investment in machines, schools, etc.); second, subsidies to improve farmers' incomes; and third, credit subsidies.

The credit subsidies category has been added because including such subsidies in "structural ameliorations" had been criticized by those who claimed that credit subsidies also had an income effect.[73]

At any rate, the classification shows that farm subsidies were only partially designed to change agricultural structure; to a great extent they have been regarded as permanent income subsidies. To indicate the trend, let us compare:

GREEN PLANS, 1956 TO 1964
Classification of subsidies according to purpose

	Structure (mill. DM)	Income	Credit
1956	250	320	46
1958	403	903	35
1960	649	767	55
1962	905	1007	224
1964	1330	959	236

If the series of subsidies had had nothing else in mind but to "adjust" German peasantry, the correct—although imprudent—title of the measure could have been "Green Plan for raising productivity by reducing agricultural units from two million to 0.7 million and the agricultural population from 25 per cent to 10 per cent of the total working population."[74] Actually, this is the effect of the Green Plan desired and expected by the majority of voters and taxpayers in Germany, although not by the farmers. This indicates the delicate political ramifications of any plan.

Spatial Planning

On October 1, 1963, the Federal Minister for Housing, City Building, and Spatial Order (Minister für Wohnungswesen, Städtebau und Raumordnung) submitted to the Bundestag a 57-page paper called "First Report of the Federal Government on Spatial Order."[75] The report was an answer to parliamentary requests dating back to the beginning of the year.

It was a demographic and ecological survey of the location of basic resources, the transport network, and the effects of international treaties on the Federal Republic (i.e., location problems posed by the Common Market), among other things. It included an analysis of the development of industry, agriculture, services, tax revenue, towns, cities, and regions. An appendix listed all measures affecting territory issued by executive branches and twelve "Laws encompassing Clauses which Regulate Spatial Problems" proposed during the legislative session. The report included sixteen charts and a great deal of statistical material. It was the work of a special group within the ministry which is mainly composed of advocates of town and country planning. It was sponsored by the minister and the Secretary of State and supported by private organizations with similar ideas from outside government.

The report was met with mixed feelings by the public and by political and governmental units. For example, it aroused deep concern among municipal politicians who feared that national spatial plans would weaken their autonomy to make their own policies—e.g., attracting industry by local tax exemption.[76] This was mainly due to the fact that the planners in the ministry had drawn various charts based on a study of ecological trends. These charts revealed concrete plans, with de- and re-concentration measures envisaged by selecting new "central regions" chosen to be especially supported, and by other "dirigistic" measures which indicated that the planners did not trust automatic market decisions.

The report was really just a compilation and integration of many existing spatial plans, although, it has to be admitted, with some "systematic" thought behind it. Under the aegis of the Federal Economic Ministry, many special measures have been under consideration with respect to particular regions, including subsidies to "emergency regions," "pivotal regions," and "boundary regions." There were always distinctly "poor" regions in the Federal Republic which required and received special assistance under a "structural policy."[77] But these regions were not spliced together into an "entire plan" covering the total area of the Federal Republic. This is now being done, and the result is another violent controversy over the problem of whether there should be "total planning" in a market economy or not. There is a fine irony in this dispute since the Minister of Housing and Spatial Order, who is his own advocate for establishing a national spatial plan, is, at the same time, the man who, against much opposition, has pushed the reliberalization of rent control.[78]

The spatial planners argue that "space," being unproduceable and irremovable, cannot be fully integrated into a market economy and needs special treatment. This has been a well-known economist's argument since Adam Smith. It must be added that in Germany the spatial "plan" as a working "chart" has a long history in administrative law, especially in municipal administration where road and block building required both a nonmarket mapping out of spatial relations and legal means for expropriation and indemnification. A conference of administrative jurists recently debated "The Plan as an Institution of Administrative Law" and devoted 99 per cent of the time to the "Raumplan"—the spatial or physical plan.[79]

The present revival of discussions on spatial planning, healthy as it may be, suffers from certain inherent limitations. Spatial planning is but one aspect of economic planning in the modern sense. The spatial planners appear somewhat sectarian when they reduce economic phenomena primarily to "space," instead of using "money" as a central measuring rod and target of a market economy. Whether there can exist a plan which places neither space nor money as the central criterion remains open to argument.

Coordinated Economic Policy

As noted earlier, federal economic policy has often been attacked for lacking a "concept." The difficulties which occur when policies need to be coordinated within the cabinet have been listed. We must now consider one of the first achievements in macroeconomic action stimulated by international cooperation: the Economic Report of the Federal Republic, prepared since 1963 according to the request of the OECD in Paris, as part of the OECD Annual Report.

A quotation from June, 1964, may be indicative of public interest in technical instruments designed to intervene in economic affairs: "The federal government requires the development of anticyclical instruments in order to make possible quicker action."[80] This demand is in the context of an analysis of the inflationary dangers seen following higher exports, lower imports, and collective bargaining in a climate of higher national liquidity.

The federal government suggested, as an anticyclical measure, the reduction of tariffs to raise imports, but this has been rejected by the Bundestag committee on foreign trade. Other counter measures proposed by the government are: additional taxation of government and other fixed-interest bonds sold to foreigners; restriction of public investment (said to make up 50 per cent of all investments) in multiannual programs; reduction of consumer purchasing power by tax increases and the freezing of money; and lowered depreciation rates.

Some of these suggestions can be carried out without explicitly changing budget law: for example, the hoarding of money or repaying debts before maturity. Other typically modern anticyclical measures require special laws. In this respect, it should be remembered that the federal constitution contains articles proscribing anticyclical measures of an expanding sort, such as deficit spending. Thus the government demands greater powers to control a boom while maintaining the limitations on the use of instruments needed to control a recession.

The federal government proposals cited above are part of a "Supplement to the Report on Economic Trends in 1963 and Prospects for 1964 (Economic Report 1964)," submitted by the Chancellor to the Bundestag in June, 1964, after consideration in the cabinet. The main report had been submitted in December, 1963.[81] This was the second report of this type; the first one had been published as a German Memorandum to the Annual Report 1963/64 of OECD. It is worthwhile, in summing up the official attitude in West Germany toward national economic programing, to quote from the English translation of the second report:

> The following survey of the overall economic situation and prospects continues the practice begun by the Economic Report 1963. Reporting of this kind will in future be a task for the independent body to be appointed under the Law of Forming a Council of Experts to Report on Overall Economic Trends, dated 14 August 1963. . . . Meanwhile the Federal Cabinet presents this Economic Report on its own responsibility. It is led to do so for the following reasons in particular.

Notwithstanding all criticism on details the first Report was well received by Parliament and the public; the Bundesrat[82] asked the Cabinet to continue this type of reporting. It was found that the preview of the economic process, the elucidating of interrelations and the clarifying of effects produced by the behavior of certain groups and institutions contributed towards rendering discussion of economic policy objective. There is some evidence that the pointing out of possible errors and dangers increased individual groups' awareness of responsibility, and improved public authorities' understanding of the results produced by their decisions. Although the guiding principles stated in the last Report were followed only in part, they do seem to have affected the actual course of economic activity in 1963. The fact that the trends were in some respects more favourable than had been feared at the beginning of 1963 was doubtless not only due to changes of objective data, but also evidently reflects greater regard for the requirements of the economy as a whole.

It seemed desirable not to enter into details or special problems. This had the great advantage that the overall economic relationships remain discernible. It is true that composite findings very often conceal differing individual movements, but there are enough reports dealing with sections of the economic process. And against the desire for the most comprehensive reporting possible there has been the no less urgent demand that the Report should be kept as short as practicable.[83]

It may suffice, then, to list the table of contents of this Report:

Economic Trends in 1963:
     Chief Results for the Year
     Trends in the Light of Economic Policy Objectives
Prospective Economic Trends in 1964:
     Initial Situation, Assumptions and Overall Survey
     Demand
     Supply
     Prices
Assessment of 1964 Economic Trends and Conclusions regarding Economic Policy:

Economic Trends and Economic Policy Objectives
Conclusions and Guiding Principles regarding Economic
Policy.[84]

The reader will easily discern that the German federal government has "made a virtue out of misfortune," as a German proverb
runs. Being obliged to comply with the rules of OECD to publish
reports on past and future economic events of a programing character, but wishing to remain within the neoliberalist doctrine and
policy practices, it produced an able mélange of verbal submission
to demand and formal maintenance of dogma.

The table of contents is illustrative. It speaks of over-all surveys,
economic trends, policy objectives, and guiding principles, all in the
vocabulary of neoliberalism. In the preface (cited above), the polite
refusal to give details is justified by pragmatic reasons (brevity,
practicability, etc.) instead of by dogmatic ones, but much is
revealed by this: "It is true that composite findings very often conceal differing individual movements, but there are enough reports
dealing with sections of the economic process." Reports dealing
with sections are usually *not* put together in an over-all format; they
continue to exist separately without any attempt to splice them
together. The pitfall of a simple presentation of over-all economic
relationships is that it leaves open the problem of how the "reports
dealing with sections" (and, to add, usually prepared *by* these
sections) are to be integrated in an over-all scheme.

But the federal government is aware of these pitfalls. It wants
to use them as warning signals to indicate that the liberalist, pluralistic market economy is still alive. The reports, so to speak, represent the ultimate possible concession toward "integrated programing" for which West German leaders are ready in times of normalcy. What will happen in times of recession or crisis is an open
question.

SUPRANATIONAL PROGRAMING

Marshall Plan and OEEC/OECD

Under the Marshall Plan and subsequent U.S. aid programs,
1.5 billion dollars were transferred to West Germany from 1948 to
1954. Under GARIOA Fund help, another 1.62 billion dollars
entered in 1946–50.[85] A special ministry was formed for the ad-

ministration of the Marshall Plan and the counterpart funds collected from the payments of importers; it was for a long time headed by the vice chancellor of the Federal Republic.

This ministry published annual reports (from 1949) on the use of counterpart funds. These to some extent with the consent of the U.S. ERP-, later MSA-Administration, had been invested mainly in housing, energy, agriculture, and basic resources. Ten per cent were regularly invested in Berlin. The Fund is registered as a "special treasury fund" (Sondervermögen) of the Federation, similar to the German Railways and other institutions. For 1964, 1.05 billion marks were spent: 472 million for Berlin aid, 200 million for foreign aid, and 378 million in aid to the West German economy.

Certainly these sums as well as other credit funds distributed through government channels, e.g., by Kreditanstalt für Wiederaufbau,[86] were placed according to macroeconomic considerations and not, as with ordinary private banks, according to the application of the credit-seeking agencies and bankers' judgments of liquidity or profitability. But these ex-ante reflections could at best be called a policy, not a program, and certainly not a plan. This is pointed up by the fact that counterpart funds can only be allocated with parliamentary consent, like any other budgetary funds of the government. Thus they become part of the ordinary legislative process and its pluralistic consequences. A real programing or planning influence could barely be detected and, to our knowledge, had never been envisaged by MSA administrators. There have been, it is true, some prognostic attempts on a European scale which could have affected German economic policy. But since the "three sage men" predicted a development of energy consumption and infra-structure which was never realized,[87] there has been no greater willingness to rely on extrapolated data coming from abroad than to accept domestic forecasts as policy signposts.

Supranational Institutions of the Six

The supranational institutions of the six are the Coal and Steel Community, the Atomic Commission, and the European Economic Community, all dating from 1951 and 1957. This preliminary study will concentrate on the Economic Community as the largest and most characteristic one.

The author admits that he was somewhat surprised when, in Paris in 1957, he was presented the "law" on the Economic Community for the first time in the shape of a timetable, i.e., a fifteen-year plan. The German version had been presented in the form of a classical "law."

However, the Act on the Economic Community has, in the course of events, more and more revealed its character as a plan. For example, as indicated earlier, it contains a fifteen-year plan for the reduction of the farm population to 10 per cent of the working population. Dates play important roles, and once on New Year's Eve a commission had to put back the clock, in order to comply with legal (i.e., chronologically planned) provisions for executing some economic movement on time.[88]

However, in Germany the Act has always been considered a measure designed as a sort of "last plan" for the community of the six. After all, the treaty forming the Economic Community has also been called the Common *Market*. There were not a few German politicians for whom even this "common market"—if established in a liberalist spirit—would have been too protectionist or *"dirigistisch"* because its scope was too small. "Smaller Europe" (*Kleineupora*), apart from being criticized for aiming at widespread political objectives, was considered to be a constricting rather than a promoting device for a world market (or half-world market). Professor Erhard, then Minister of Economics, was rather skeptical about the project and declared publicly on various occasions that he would vote for it only out of political necessity, since economically the treaty was pure nonsense. The Liberal party faction in Parliament (being super-classical in economic policy in some respects) voted against it.

The actual performance of the treaty provisions has not eliminated suspicions—not only those of President de Gaulle. Misgivings expressed against the Common Market from within the Federal Republic are based on three observations.

First, instead of, or in addition to, developing "more markets" among the Six, there is (also) more supra-government bureaucracy. "Will Brussels mean the end of our market economy?" is a question which makes headlines in financial newspapers.[89] Individual businessmen, lawyers, and special pleaders of interest groups acknowledge that the High Commission and its officials have started to "govern" already by sending representatives and lobbyists to their High Commission headquarters. They learn at the same time that a supranational bureaucracy is more difficult to penetrate and make accessible than a national one.

Second, it is realized that the treaty provisions, as well as practical developments, tend to establish a real supranational authority above the national government. This was a declared aim of those who, for political reasons, supported the EEC—and it is, to say the least, an open question what kind of economic policy this authority will, in the last instance, carry out. There is evidence that the French will play a major role in shaping the emerging policy.

And this leads to the third cause of suspicion: the Commission made it quite clear in 1962 that it had "programs" for the future. In July, 1962, a report was published concerning "the execution of the treaty (January, 1958—January, 1962)" under the subtitle: "The first phase of the Common Market" (*Erste Stufe des Gemeinsamen Marktes*).[90] This phrasing indicated nothing more than strict compliance with treaty provisions and meant that the next step was to follow. The first four years were not much more than a realization of a (not yet completed) tariff union. What was to follow really meant the institution of a common *policy*. In October, 1962, the Commission published a "Memorandum concerning the Action Program of the Community for the Second Phase."[91] There the word was: "program."

This program turned out to be no more than a series of "should" and "ought to" reflections on various "common policies" of the Community: transport, energy, foreign currency, foreign aid, administration, and finance, with liberalist policies on the "free flow of goods, labor, capital" and "competition" presented in the first two chapters among eleven. However, the section on economic policy contained a point, "long-term programing" (*längerfristige Vorausschau*), number 104 of which read as follows: "The Commission, therefore, intends to submit to the Council by mid-1963, proposals in the direction of a joint-programing (*gemeinschaftliche Programmierung*)."[92]

An open encounter followed between Professor Hallstein (president of the Commission) and Professor Erhard (then federal Minister of Economics). Erhard said that "we must not allow centralistic tendencies to come up in our economic policy," and

Hallstein replied that "we have not, with this program, opened the way for what many people understand as a planned economy (Plan-wirtschaft); this programing is not identical with a plan which would restrict the freedom of the market and would be enforced upon the private enterprise; it is comparable to a frame. . . ." The economic shadow minister of the Social Democrats sided with Hallstein, former "Roman" law professor, once Secretary of State in the Ministry of Foreign Affairs and intimate collaborator of Konrad Adenauer.[93]

In the meantime, the public debate has switched somewhat from the economic aspect of the Community to the political.[94] Great Britain's application for admittance, General de Gaulle's refusal and the less than integrationalist course of the French chief of state have revived the original political motives behind the economic mechanism in Brussels.

But the economic machinery has been put in motion, and it does not seem that French neo-nationalism will stall this machine to save German neoliberalism. Rather, the neomercantilism of the very able French bureaucracy may outwit both. At any rate, the caustic prophecy of the former president of the Association of German Chambers of Industry and Commerce will probably prove false: "The idea that Europe means adding the precision of the French laws to the precision of the German civil service official is a night-mare."[95]

Preliminary Appraisal

The reader will have noticed that we did not offer a definition of planning until the end of our study. It runs: "Planning—drawing up a timetable of prescribed actions, the enacting of which by the joint efforts of a multitude will produce by technical necessity a desired effect." This is surely one of the most rigid definitions one could choose. The reason why we selected it is to make crystal clear that, notwithstanding all mixed systems and sliding scales, one has to cross a Rubicon in order to reach planning or programing from the standpoint of a competitive money economy. First, there must be logico-systematic integration of the actions of individual agents to serve a common end, and, second, there must be "enactment" of these actions. The motive need not necessarily be obedience to orders; it may be compliance with monetary lures. But even if monetary lures are applied, there ought to be no talk of planning unless a definite, clearly described, economic objective is first set forth as a *common* goal, which can be realized only by common effort, and second, this objective is really *willed* by those responsible for enacting the plan.

To call something an economic plan which is the chance result of hazardous actions committed by a multitude of individuals who are spliced together by a Law of Great Numbers or by strategic behavior according to the Theory of Games will not help to clarify issues. A competitive economy may be a good device to produce indefinable but desired results under given circumstances, but certainly this by itself is not economic planning.

116

HISTORICAL SETTING

To recapitulate briefly, the West German population has an ambiguous memory of national economic planning. It has known planned economies during two world wars and next door in the Soviet Union and the Soviet Zone of Germany in peacetime. In all these cases, planning finally resulted in organized scarcity. Whether this was cause or effect, whether it expresses an observation which could be generalized, is of little concern to the collective memory.

On the other hand, it was a planned economy which dragged the Germans out of the Great Depression and provided work for six million unemployed, whereas a system very similar to the one now claiming approval in West Germany (Neoliberalism) proved incapable of solving the problem of mass unemployment.

At present, collective memory relies on the most recent experience, which is the "marvelous" reconstruction of the West German economy after World War II. It has been realized by a non-planned economy, or stated even more strongly, by an economic system which emphatically regards itself as *anti*-planning. This system has brought a remarkable rise in the living standards of a great majority of the people—even when compared with prewar and pre-depression levels. The majority tend to attribute this capacity to the system for all times and all other circumstances. Neoliberalism is even linked with parliamentarian democracy as representing the two basic prerequisites for a free society.

The different generations in West Germany have a slightly different attitude when judging the economic structure. The difference depends on how (at which age, in which role) they have experienced the various "historical marginal situations" of the nation: World War I, the Big Inflation of 1923, the Great Depression, the National Socialist Third Reich, and World War II. The unspecified ideological incrustation of non-planning or anti-planning which became prevalent in public discussion, amounting to almost a new "book religion" with prophets (Röpke, Rüstow) and preachers (Erhard, Müller-Armack), may be partially because of too much re-education (a sort of renegade's fanaticism), partially an expression of a kind of *ersatz* nationalism opposing French Cartesianism and Russian proletarianism.

Most remarkably, almost all the lessons of the once famous and flourishing "German School of Historical Political Economy" (Fr. List, Max Weber, Schmoller, Sombart, etc.) seem to be forgotten. New aspects of the same line of thought are being imported from abroad via W. W. Rostow[1] and others. There is, officially, little reflection on potential correlations between economic stages and economic systems.

Experience proved after World War II that the market principle is a suitable means to be used in reconstructing an already developed, highly industrialized economy which was badly destroyed. Whether it is also suitable for any other environmental setting remains to be seen, but this kind of relativistic question is rarely asked in West Germany. If it is asked, it is not in connection with their own situation but in regard to foreign underdeveloped countries. All major groups in the West German economy want to be left free and "autonomous," and practically all believe that planning of any sort is incompatible with this freedom. Even labor unions and Social Democrats are hesitant to trade their bargaining freedom for a controlled economy. It is quite clear that business subscribes to statements such as: "A planning program which would try to influence free entrepreneurial and individual decisions by means other than those compatible with democracy and the Rule of Law (*demokratischer Rechtsstaat*), is rejected without discussion; just the same happens with the idea to exert sanctions upon behavior inconsistent with a plan."[2]

RATIONALIZING ECONOMIC POLICY

The same body of industrial managers whose fierce rejection of over-all planning was just referred to continues to consider three different techniques as legitimate within the context of a market economy:

(1) projections (of over-all economic development)
(2) prognoses (forecasting of the effect of specific economic policy measures)
(3) economic planning for government-operated sectors excluded from the market process (such as agriculture, transportation, energy, road construction, etc.)

Whereas planning within the public sector is sometimes considered compatible with a market economy even when it includes rigid budgeting and compulsory operations (on the part of governmental agents), programing within the private sector is strictly limited to noncompulsory, purely "indicative" recommendations. It is explicitly stated that any relation between the prognosis and the result occurs only by chance under the present conditions of economic organization.

Planning the government-controlled sectors (comprising about 40 per cent of the GNP) is often demanded by both left and right wing advocates, who want to reduce the contradictions among various governmental agents. But very little has been done. First, it is realized that effective planning of the government-controlled sector would imply integration of all governmental agents (on all levels), against which at least one obstacle seems unsurmountable, the federal character of the Republic. Second, doubts are raised whether 60 per cent of an economy can be left to competitive markets when 40 per cent is controlled by one agent.

Others, when talking of "planning the governmental sector," mean something quite different from coordinating and budgeting the existing government-controlled economic agents: they demand something which is often called "rationalizing economic policy." This is the same thing which was described above as "prognosis," meaning to predict the effects of, and select the right instruments for, particular economic policy objectives. This is a demand which seemingly even purists cannot frown upon. It is quite legitimate if somebody who acts wants to know in advance the scope and strength of his techniques.

It is here that the role of the "expert" comes in, namely the expert in macroeconomics who tries to predict the effects of alternative policy measures. Such experts have entered the government and already play an important role in developing the technique of decision-making, although they do not share political responsibility for the decisions. The Permanent Expert Council attached to the Ministry of Economics, for example, has recommended middle-range national economic programing designed to "rationalize policy." Erhard's successor as Minister of Economics, Schmücker, seems to be less dogmatic regarding this type of "coordination" than the present Chancellor and his former Secretary of State, Müller-Armack, used to be.

But in West Germany (as well as in the United States), "the state of economic science," as proclaimed by the most renowned among the economists, has been acutely analyzed: "Discounting this unlikely possibility [namely, of two countries or two periods starting from identical situations, but applying two different policies], the ability to predict the effect of policies cannot be tested separately from straight forecasting performance."[3]

This means, predicting a single policy effect presupposes over-all macroeconomic forecasting techniques, but functioning macro-economic prediction is just what is considered incompatible with the free play of market forces which make a predicted result come about only by chance.

We have to ask the sober question why public authorities and private agents still occupy themselves with sharpening macroeco-nomic tools when their application seems, in the last instance, not wanted.

Economic science in West Germany—as elsewhere—finds it-self little prepared to meet the demands of the most ardent of the planning champions. But it also seems to be overburdened when asked to help those most cautious politicians who only want to rationalize economic policies. In our estimation, what they are looking for is an economic policy technique which produces desired results without hurting basic neoliberalist principles. In other words, rational progress is desired, but without crossing the Rubicon. Planning an unplanned society is the aim, and this means, in the last instance, fortifying this side of the Rubicon by applying means which can only be harvested by crossing it. Translated into eco-nomic language, one shuns issuing commands to individual eco-nomic agents but looks for monetary or other devices to produce the same effect as a command would produce, without really com-manding anybody. Instead of "planning" the neoliberalists speak, in this instance, of "control" (*Steuerung*).

It is the economic expert who is, and feels, charged with finding the economic policy tools which can be applied without affecting the commercial principle of a market society; in other words, find-ing methods for influencing people and producing desired actions without depriving these same people of the convictions that they act on their own rational autonomy. Or in still other words, to make people cooperate while maintaining their belief that they are competing against each other.

Some of the commercial agents of the competitive economy who, on the one hand, jealously guard their autonomy of action are, on the other hand, quite willing to join this cooperative game. Thus some industrial associations favor the French planning system because it "produces a clearing of ideas and helps foster a climate of confidence among business, public administration, and even labor,"[4] but certainly not because it switches the control method of the economic process from competition to planning. Others consider the expert designs to be dangerous Trojan planning horses in the liberal stable, notwithstanding the experts' assertion that monetary control instruments are not commands. For these critics the modern expert, bureaucrat, or technocrat simply has replaced the former Socialist as the arch enemy. However, these critics may not be in principle opposed to *any* sort of cooperation among economic agents. It is among them that one finds stern advocates of cartel practices and outspoken opponents to government anticartel legislation and jurisdiction.

In West Germany "rationalizing economic policy" is the concept which occupies the place taken in other Western countries by "national economic planning." Here, as there, we find the procedure presented as a technical instrument designed, or at least looked for, by experts claiming objectivity. On the other hand, the potential scientific objectivity of the macroeconomic process is disputed by those who stress the political element.

POLITICAL WILL VERSUS EXPERT OBJECTIVITY

It is certainly a difficult task for experts to search for and develop modern instruments for forecasting and predicting economic processes and/or the effects of economic policy techniques. But much more difficult is the actual use of these instruments once they have been found suitable to produce predictable ends. Neither the tools nor the ends will be approved by all those people who are needed as collaborators.

The West German lesson is clear: macroeconomic planning is not a technological but a political issue. It is a matter of will rather than of knowledge, or, more precisely, of knowledge that is useless without will. Once more we have to quote the present Minister of Economics, Schmücker, then a member of parliament, rebuffing Social Democratic economics professors during the debate on family allowances: "We shall not sacrifice our political will, not even to the arguments of greater expert knowledge."[5]

The attempt to carry out any planning scheme introduced into West Germany has been broken by the political power of special interests. If its macroeconomic effects can be predetermined, they will be clear not only to the experts involved, but also to the microeconomic agents who will be the inevitable losers in the deal; someone must be the loser whenever there is economic change. Once negative effects of this sort are known, a parliament (or other legislative body) composed of members of the commercial market cannot ignore opposing votes which may, on critical issues, change from opposition to resistance.

Moreover, who can ordain planning procedures in an economy that has just experienced a miraculous boom by a modern version of laissez faire? Politically, any overt extension of programing or planning schemes is less feasible now than it has ever been. All attempts to sell planning as a more effective and efficient technique than simple competition (even if only consisting of assertions that already existing techniques deemed compatible with market procedures "could be interpreted as planning") are doomed to failure in view of the distress produced by economic planning in the Soviet bloc countries or of the West-East contrast in standards of living.

Furthermore, in continental Europe the main argument in favor of economic planning has never been one of efficiency but one emerging from the teachings of political philosophy, political justice, and political order. Economic planning, like political democracy, was presented as a tool of political progress helping to do away with feudal suppression, state dominance, and arbitrary rule. This was the way the Co-Determination Law, introduced in West Germany in 1951, was advocated by the unions and Social Democrats. The Marxist heritage was still alive to that extent, and it may reappear again as soon as material circumstances are less favorable to the simple tactics of "more and more and more" money, now practiced by the unions. Recently there have been attempts to revive the old claim for "co-determination in technical production, work rules and assembly line speed" in collective bargaining; the demands were justified by the slogan "the humanization of labor."[6] This is neither efficiency nor humanism, but pure politics—the question of "who shall decide."

But it has grown uncertain whether pure politics will, under present circumstances, be capable of reintroducing the issue of economic planning as an issue of democratic progress into West German discussion. This political argument has lost impact since economic efficiency and the standard of living have replaced self-determination as the principles of political legitimacy. And here we are back again to what we just said: in competing for efficiency, planning systems, as they have been seen until now, are considered by West Germans to be hopelessly behind in the material race. People subscribe to the economic system which brings them well-being, without listening to arguments which point out its alleged political inferiority. This is a source of grave disappointment to all radical leftists, including the late Dr. Victor Agartz, former chief economic consultant of the Federation of Labor Unions.

In the present state of domestic and foreign policy in West Germany, there is no group that might call for planning, either in the name of political justice or of economic efficiency, which could rally the substantial majority to support the conversion of economic principles necessary for the dangerous experiment. A majority different from the one presently governing could always shift emphasis in the circulation of income; extend the use of propaganda, of influence on speculation, and of mass persuasion; change the economic style; and redirect the policy makers. But this would not alter the essence of the system: to control by trial, error, probability, and bargaining, not by planning.

As to the macroeconomic experts, technocrats, and technicians of economic control: If they do not remain simply, as Montesquieu said of the third branch of government, the judiciary, "en quelque façon nuls," they suffer an even less honorable fate. Claiming objectivity for their comments on macroeconomic movements and yet having to admit the hazardous nature of the system, they are in danger of being labeled special pleaders and may lose their suprapartisan credibility. One of these two developments has happened to almost every one of the experts who entered the political scene in West Germany. Macroeconomic expertise added to a business society did not result in "democratic planning" or in any such "third force" system. The best thing that has happened to the experts was that they turned out to be good businessmen, i.e., good salesmen of their ideas.

THE MIXED SYSTEM

Many of the middle-of-the-road designers of economic systems in West Germany have tried to make believe that simply by coining new words they could get business to accept planning more readily. One of the most promising debates among businessmen and experts on economic planning was published with a foreword written by one of the experts. There we read: "The new concepts—'prognosis,' 'programing,' 'planning'—could not be classified under the categories 'socialist'/ 'liberalist,'/ or 'compulsory system'/ 'market system,' by which thinking about economic policy has been fixed in the Federal Republic. . . . In the Federal Republic, too, we do not have a pure competitive economy, but a mixed economic system."[7] There again is the mixed system.

The only apparent difference between this mixed system, as known in West Germany and elsewhere in the West, and a business system pure and simple is that within a mixed system not only goods and services are priced and traded but planning also. There is one more commodity on the market, macroeconomic programs (including those designed by government).

The ideological fog hovering over West Germany does not stem so much from leftists and rightists in the strict sense but from "in-betweens," those who assert that everything in the West German economy is already well on the way to a third system; but this is not true. National planning for increased individual consumption, and hence for increased individual production, may become technically possible. But it is hard to see how, given the present state of mind in the Federal Republic and among its more potent allies, it can become politically feasible now. When on the other hand, economic planning becomes politically feasible in Germany, individual consumption may not be its main objective.

It may be that in an affluent society national planning will no longer impinge on individual freedom, as it does in the economic systems of scarcity which are, up to the present, the Germans' sole experience with planned economies or "rationalized economic poli-

PRELIMINARY APPRAISAL 125

cies." It may then be that the elaboration and execution of economic planning will be *demanded* and *controlled* by the people in the sense that it "demands and controls," today, the elaboration and execution of a railroad timetable, because individual plans will be made secure by the carrying out of macroeconomic plans. Nobody, then, will feel that his autonomy, his freedom, is restricted by punctual execution of economic plans (even if they regulate a part of his own actions), just as nobody today feels restricted in his freedom because he has to comply with consumer-oriented timetables in the transportation systems.

The author is prepared to argue that *in this sense* the West German economy could already be called a "mixed system," i.e., there are many demands for timetable security voiced by all sorts of groups, not only employees and workmen, but entrepreneurs as well. The more saturation is approached, the more even minor irregularities in quality, quantity, income, prices, and deliveries of goods and services are resented.

But what is here termed a mixed economy is not what is meant by those who usually use this word. The fact that subsections of the population "desire" objectives that would require, for realization, aggregate actions of a multitude (such as stable money), does not yet alter the essence of the system. In West Germany this system is against all mixed versions. It is still dominated by the concepts of risk, uncertainty, and profit, and these are the concepts of a market economy and of its corresponding actors, goods, and services. A new service has been added to the assorted supply: macroeconomic forecasts, techniques, and programs. But they are, like all other goods and services, produced and offered, sold and bought, and demanded and consumed by partisans of special interests.

It may be that these instruments of macroeconomics would be much better suited to regulating an economy of nonpartisans who cooperate for common goals instead of competing for private motives. And perhaps the functioning of national economic planning in West Germany would not even require a major change in organizational technology (which has already happened), but could work with "only" a change in the motives and understanding of the participants.

But it is a fact that neither such motives nor such understanding underlies economic psychology in West Germany. No foolproof test has been developed so far to find out, for practical purposes, where and how to produce what we have called "supra-partisan credibility." This credibility—the "objectivity" of the expert viewed as a political phenomenon—is a prerequisite for the elaboration and execution of economic programing for supra-partisan objectives. Where there is no such credibility, economic planning suggestions will always be seen as especially clever and tricky devices to outwit others in the competitive struggle. This, to conclude, is the secret belief of the West German veterans of politics and business (though perhaps not of science), and of labor and government, though they may not be happy with it. In Chapter IV of this preliminary study we tried to show how this belief has worked out. We also tried to show that the younger generation (of all the political and economic groups) is trying to reintroduce a new-old *"non omnis confundar"* to counter the resignation of the elder businessmen, statesmen, and workmen.

The simple description of events, procedures, and actions which make up this study may serve to suggest tentative answers to the question of whether national economic planning in West Germany has to be "made," if the people will it, or can simply be called out of hiding.

PERSPECTIVES

Our tentative answer will include at least one assertion: National economic planning will, under present political circumstances in West Germany, never mean "making individual economic agents obey precalculated and prescribed data for the future course of the economy, fabricated by any 'third force,' such as macroeconomic experts inside or outside the government." However, it seems as if economic planning is understood in this mistaken way by most social forces in West Germany.

This misconception seriously hampers even debating the issue in the Federal Republic. Both management and labor (and many others) think that "planning" means breaking the free and reasonable will of the individual economic agent. To divert them from their idea it will perhaps be necessary to introduce entirely new terms, avoiding the term "plan" which has become discredited beyond correction.

It should be made clear that the use of compulsion to attain targets is not the essential feature of integrated planning and that such planning does not eliminate "risk" on the part of those who are responsible for formulation and execution. The principal characteristics of planning on a national scale are cooperation and integration, just as with planning in an individual firm. This cooperation and integration can be effected by mutual consent and contract, instead of by force and coercion "from a neutral power above." If done this way, it does not break the free will of the parties concerned but *enlarges* the field of free and reasonable action, without trying to remove, by decree, potential failure.

Enlarging the field for reasonable action means enlarging the field of security. The demand for greater security (e.g., against unemployment, depression, inflation) is the main motive for demanding national economic planning. Now, a people can never have more security than it and its neighbors are willing to bring about by their own actions. This applies to economics as well as to foreign policy. Hence, since security can be realized by agreement, it must be possible to institute economic planning by contract between free (autonomous) and reasonable (profit-seeking) partners. The decisive difference between such contracts and ordinary business bargains is that the partners must have an objective in common which transcends the individual (e.g., profit) motive, without necessarily impeding it.

Unless the common objective is desired by all concerned, including international trade partners abroad, there can be no national economic planning. There is, indeed, a growing series of common objectives (such as full employment, monetary stability, steady economic growth) emerging despite conflicting interests, but this process is far from finished in West Germany. On the international scene, little more than lip service is paid to these objectives.

If the West German population could be induced to accept as "planning" cooperating and integrating procedures which aim at these common objectives, many would lose their suspicions of macroeconomic experts. It is within the context of such procedures that they will obtain their proper place, a place very similar to that held by the judiciary in a liberal society.

The macroeconomic expert derives his standing from a suprapartisan credibility which makes him a "specialist in generalities," i.e., an expert on *common* objectives and procedures for their realization. This is the sort of veto knowledge he can rightly claim. But unless the economy becomes one "regulated from above or from the outside," the expert's veto has to be restrained to the field of *knowledge* (technology): the expert cannot assume will or power, because he does not represent a social force. In that respect, he remains as neutral in politics as a physician treating a patient or an engineer constructing a bridge.

We are faced here with two hard facts: political action cannot be achieved by the execution of technical designs or by the perfection of technical processes, and so-called "neutral expertise" has little political appeal, nor can "experts" ever become a political force. The political aversion to the acceptance of planning, which is so widespread in West Germany, may be due to this very fact that planning has mostly been advocated and launched by "technically minded" spirits.

★★★

Appendix

STRUCTURAL DEVELOPMENT OF THE GERMAN ECONOMY

(Source: *Statistical Yearbook of Federal Republic*)
Absolute figures of 1938 reduced to Federal Republic territory.

	1938	1952	1961
I. NATIONAL PRODUCT, ITS FORMATION AND DISTRIBUTION			
GNP in Billion Deutsche Mark			
or Reichsmark (1 DM = $0.25)	47.9 (1936)	126.0	310.4
Exports in per cent of GNP (19.6 in 1913)	6.4	13.4	23.9
Private consumption in per cent of domestic GNP	60.5	57.5	58.2
Government	20.8	18.4	14.2
Gross private and public investment of domestic GNP	18.7	24.1	27.5
Workers' wages and employees salaries in per cent of national income	54.9	57.9	62.3
II. GOVERNMENTAL BUDGETS			
All government, public, and para-fiscal budgets in per cent of GNP	18.3	39.9	35.6
Taxes and contributions to parafiscal agents, p. cap.	379	910	1970
Direct taxes (on revenue, property, income, etc.) in per cent of all tax revenue	——	55.3	57.5
In per cent of all govt. budgets (soc. security not included):			
Regular administration costs	40.8	30.0	29.2
Formation of capital (incl. investment)	17.3	26.3	20.7
Transfers of income and capital	18.9	30.3	40.3
Defense, occupation, and war charges	23.0	13.4	9.8

129

	1938	1952	1961
III. OCCUPATIONAL STRUCTURE			
Active population in millions	20.0	22.5	25.3
In per cent of active population:			
(in per cent of all labor force in parenth.):			
Agriculture, forestry, and fishing (primary sector):	27	23	14.3
	(7.2)	(6.6)	(2.8)
Industry (second sector):	42	45	48.7
	(54.8)	(56.4)	(59.5)
Trade, transport, and service (tertiary sector):	31	32	36.8
	(34.9)	(34.2)	(37.7)
In per cent of active population:			
Independent business and profession	14.9	14.8	12.7
Labor force	66.7	70.8	76.6
Employees (1939/1950/1961)	13.2	16.0	23.0
Govt. officials at all levels (1939/1950/1961)	5.1	4.0	4.7
Per cent of employees organized in unions	——	15.7	12.3
Per cent of workers organized in unions	——	39.3	40.5
IV. BUSINESS STRUCTURE			
Total figure of agricultural enterprise units (in mio.)	2.04	2.017	1.727
Agricultural units covering more than 5 hectar (about 12½ acres) in millions (1938 Reich territory)	1.629	0.790	0.773
The latter dispose of ... % of total cultivated area	86.7	81.5	89.2
Total figure of enterprise units in millions (agriculture excluded)	1.956	2.131	——
Independent artisan enterprises	——	876700	756300
Industrial enterprise units (construct. not incl.)	——	92009	94205
Per cent of industrial enterprise employing less than 50 men	——	78.5	75.2
Per cent of industrial enterprise employing more than 500 men	——	2.6	2.9
Per cent of total working force employed by the latter	——	47.2	52.9
Per cent of total turnover made by the latter	——	50	——
Of total figure of enterprise units (agriculture excluded) there were:			
Shareholding companies	——	2559	——
they employed ... million men	——	2.02	——
Companies with limited liability	——	20094	——
they employed ... million men	——	1.406	——

	1938	1952	1961
V. INCOME STRUCTURE			
Per capita in Deutsche Mark or Reichsmark (until 1948)			
Population	992	1505	4459
Active population	1841	3250	9555
Independent business, profession, profits	——	5566	11522
Labor force	1771	2844	6717
Male industrial employee (1950/61)	——	4529	7344
Male industrial worker	——	4368	6878
Income in industry	——	——	6862
Income in public service	——	——	9096
Income in agriculture	——	——	4453
Per cent of independent businessmen and professions:			
Earning more than 12,000 DM annually	——	11.5	23.3
Earning less than 6,000 DM annually	——	61.2	41.5
Per cent of working force			
Earning more than 12,000 DM annually (workers)	——	0.36	1
Earning more than 12,000 DM annually (employees)	——	——	17
Earning less than 6,000 DM annually (workers)	——	95.5	31
Earning less than 6,000 DM annually (employees)	——	——	25
VI. CAPITAL FORMATION			
Gross capital formation in billion DM	——	34.4	85.6
In per cent of GNP	——	23.9	27.5
Financing of capital formation in per cent by:			
Private household saving	——	20.0	30.3
Reinvested profits of enterprise (self-financing)	——	48.6	27.8
Surpluses of govt. budgets	——	30.5	46.5
Financing of private investment in per cent by:			
Reinvested profits (self-financing)	——	41.7	——
Long- and middle-term bank credits	——	25.6	——
Short-term bank credits	——	11.3	
Issue of bonds and shares	——	2.6	——

Notes

I. Historical Roots and Reasons

1. Naturally there are decisive differences between "Bonn" and "Weimar," as will become clearer later on. Cf. F. Allemann, *Bonn ist nicht Weimar* (Cologne, 1956).

2. For the Communists in Russia and Germany at that time, see Ruth Fischer, *Stalin und der deutsche Kommunismus* (Frankfurt/M., 1950); and Leonhard Schapiro, *Die Geschichte der kommunistischen Partei der Sowjetunion* (deutsch, Frankfurt/M., 1961).

3. For the working of the Reichswirtschaftsrat (Reich Economic Council), see Chap. V.

4. First *"Mieterschutzgesetzgebung"* (Tenants' Protection) in 1923 (*Mieterschutzgesetz* of June 1, 1923, *RGBl.* I, S. 353). For partial abrogation of this legislation, see Chap. II.

5. Both coal and potash cartels were dissolved by military government decree after World War II, but other forms of administration continued to exist (see below, Chaps. II and V).

6. For the liberal course of Social Democracy, see the Godesberg Program of the German Social Democrats, of Nov. 15, 1959, quoted in the context of historical developments by *Der Weg des Sozialismus, Quellen und Dokumente,* Selected and ed. by Farner and Pinkus, *Rowohlt Deutsche Encyklopädie* (Hamburg, 1964), pp. 189–90.

7. John M. Keynes, *Allgemeine Theorie der Beschäftigung, des Zinses und des Geldes* (deutsch Berlin, 1955, 1st ed., 1936); Robert Nöll von der Nahmer, *Der volkswirtschaftliche Kreditfonds* (Berlin, 1934); C. Föhl, *Geldschöpfung und Wirtschaftskreislauf,* (Munich and Leipzig, 1937).

8. Reported by Schacht himself, in *76 Jahre Meines Lebens, Bad Wörnishofe* (1953), pp. 371, 381, 401.

9. For an appraisal of Schacht's policy by contemporaries of his time, see Maurice de Saint-Jean, *La Politique économique et financière du Troisième Reich, L'Oeuvre du Docteur Schacht* (Paris, 1936), mildly critical; Emile Roche (later president of the Conseil Economique of the French Republic), *L'Or n'est plus Roi* (Paris, 1942), enthusiastic, with a mildly reserved foreword by J. Caillaux, former French Minister of Finance.

10. Robert Nöll von der Nahmer, *Vom Werden des neuen Zeitalters* (Heidelberg, 1957), p. 274. For a systematic appraisal, see René Erbe, *Die national-sozialistische Wirtschaftspolitik 1933–1939 im Lichte der modernen Theorie* (Zurich, 1958).

134   WEST GERMANY

11. For the history of this term, see Armin Mohler, *Die konservative Revolution in Deutschland 1918–1932* (Stuttgart, 1950). For a philosophico-historical analysis of fascism, see Ernst Nolte, *Der Faschismus in seiner Epoche* (Munich, 1963).

12. H. G. Schacht, *"Währung und Wirtschaft,"* paper read at Düsseldorf, Jan. 8, 1925, printed, S. 23; Schacht, *Grundsätze deutscher Wirtschafts-politik* (Oldenburg, 1932), S. 22. See also the book of Norbert Mühlen, published in emigration: *Der Zauberer, Leben und Anleihen des Dr. H. H. G. Schacht* (Zurich, 1938), S. 5: "Dr. Hjalmar Schacht will enter history as one of those who have destroyed the institution of money."

13. Heinz Raspini, *Wirtschaftspolitik und Friede,* in *Werkhefte,* 17, Jgg., Heft 12 (Dec. 1963), Munich. See also G. W. F. Hallgarten, *Hitler, Reichs-wehr und Industrie* (Frankfurt/M., 1962); and Louis P. Lochner, *Tycoons and Tyrant: German Industry from Hitler to Adenauer* (Chicago, 1954).

14. Proclaimed on Jan. 20, 1934, followed by the decree of Oct. 20, 1934.

15. A classified memorandum issued by Hitler in 1936 on the Four Year Plan made this clear: "Therefore I demand the following targets to be reached: I. The German army must be ready for use in four years. II. The German economy must be ready for war in four years." See *Der National-sozialismus, Dokumente 1933–1945,* ed. and comment by Walther Hofer, Fischer Books, p. 172, (Frankfurt/M., 1957), p. 86.

16. For the memorandum of the Reichsbank Direktorium of January 7, 1939, which opposed Hitler and led to the break, see Annex to W. Vocke, *Gesundes Geld,* 2nd ed. (Frankfurt/M., 1956).

17. Whether non-acceptance of economic liberalism and individualism necessarily means *"The Road to Serfdom"* (Hayek, German trans. Erlenbach/Zurich, 1945) and totalitarianism is an open question. Analyses of totalitarianism usually show that it is rooted in factors other than economic variables and that central economic control may then be a consequence of totalitarianism. See C. J. Friedrich and Z. K. Brzezinski, *Totalitarian Dictatorship and Autocracy* (Cambridge, 1956); H. Arendt, *The Origins of Totalitarianism* (New York, 1951); Ernst Nolte, *Der Faschismus in Seiner Epoche.*

II. After the 1948 Currency Reform

1. Allied Control Commission, Act no. 61, 62, 63, of June 20, 27, 1948. See also Harmening and Duden, *Die Währungsgesetze* (Munich and Berlin, 1949, Supplement 1950).

2. U.S. and British Mil. Gov. Decree of March 1, 1948, on creation of Bank Deutscher Länder; June 10, 1948, effective since March 25, for French Zone, Decree of French Mil. Gov.

3. For the elimination of political constraints on markets, see Röpke, *"Wirtschaftssystem und internationale Ordnung, Prolegomena,"* in *ORDO,* Bd. 4 (Bad Godesberg, 1951), pp. 273–74.

4. The opinions were not homogeneous. Although the Labour party in Great Britain favored the German Left, occupation authorities cancelled, in 1947, a Resolution of the Landtag (diet) of North Rhine-Westphalia to expropriate the coal mines.

5. For these events, see the later report of Erhard in his book written for the 1957 election campaign, *Wohlstand für Alle* (Düsseldorf, 1957), pp. 22, 23.

6. *Ibid.*, p. 33.

7. For the Godesberg Program of SPD, see note 6, Chap. I. The book quoted there gives examples of preceding SPD programs. See also M. G. Lange, G. Schulz, K. Schütz *et al.*, *Parteien in der Bundesrepublik, Schriften des Instituts für Politische Wissenschaft* (Berlin, Stuttgart, and Düsseldorf, 1955), for a history of West German political parties (p. 90, CDU Program).

8. This is the translation used by K.-H. Hansmeyer, *Der Weg zum Wohlfahrtsstaat* (Frankfurt/M., 1957), p. 34.

9. For systematic description see Chap. III. Here we only quote the programatic book of one of the creators of the concept and system, A. Müller-Armack, *Wirtschaftslenkung und Marktwirtschaft* (Hamburg, 1948).

10. This is a basic prerequisite of all neoliberalist government intervention. The term *"marktkonform"* varies in its exact meaning; see Müller-Armack, *ibid.*, p. 93.

11. "Monetary control, unlike most direct regulations of supply, demand, and price, is impersonal and non-discriminatory," says H. S. Ellis, "The Rediscovery of Money," in *Money, Trade and Economic Growth* (New York, 1951), p. 260.

12. "Gesetz über Leitsätze für die Bewirtschaftung und Preispolitik nach der Geldreform," June 24, 1948, publ. in *Gesetzesund Verordnungsblatt des Wirtschaftsrates des Vereinigten Wirtschaftsgebietes* (July 7, 1948).

13. June 20, 1948, *Einkommensteuer-Ergänzungs-Verordnung* Control Commission Act No. 64.

14. Nov. 3, 1948, *Gesetz zur Aufhebung des Lohnstops.*

15. A slight recession facilitated removal of what remained of rationing, "It need not be mentioned that this appearance of a buyers' market was very useful in order to throw overboard the last nonsensical bit of rationing and price control."—Erhard, *op. cit.*, p. 47.

16. May 3, 1950, *Einkommensteuer-Verordnung (BGBl.* 1950, Nr. 18, p. 107).

17. July 27, 1957, *Gesetz gegen Wettbewerbsbeschränkungen (BGBl.* 1957, I, p. 1081), also called *"Kartellgesetz."*

18. See *Geschäftsbericht der Deutschen Bundesbank* for 1958, p. 72–73.

19. For Parliamentary decision concerning Preussag, see July 29, 1959, *Drucksachen-Nr.* 1228, 3. *Wahlperiode.*

20. June 23, 1960, *Gesetz über den Abbau der Wohnungszwangswirtschaft und über ein soziales Miet- und Wohnrecht (BGBl.* I, p. 389).

21. July 21, 1960, *Gesetz über die Überführung der Anteilsrechte an der Volkswagenwerk-Gesellschaft* mbH. in private hands (*BGBl.* I, p. 585).

22. Treaty constituting the Montanunion signed on Apr. 18, 1951. Ratified by West German Parliament on Apr. 29, 1952, (*BGBl.* II, p. 445).

23. Treaty constituting the Common Market signed in Rome, on Mar. 25, 1957. Ratified by the West German Parliament on July 27, 1957 (*BGBl.* II, p. 753).

24. See Erhard, *op. cit.*, p. 30. *Enrichissez-vous,* catchword of the Guizot administration in France after 1830, is usually interpreted somewhat cynically. Actually it was followed by " ... *par l'épargne et le travail"*; in this sense we quote it.

25. For details of Marshall Plan impact on West Germany see Chap. V.

26. For statistics on financing process, see Appendix.

27. The situation became worse by the social security reform (see note 56 below), which linked public pensions to an index of wage and productivity, whereas private life insurance contracts, for instance, remain without protection against inflation; indeed, legal provisions (Art. 3 of the Currency Act of 1948) prohibit indexation in any private contracts.

28. Since economic success was linked to neoliberalism, neoliberalism was linked to Professor Erhard, Erhard was linked to the Christian Democrats (or, rather to their Bavarian counterpart CSU which he joined after the FDP—Liberal party—had made him director of bizonal economy in 1948), it was Adenauer's party which got the votes cast as a sublime *plébiscite du ventre* for Erhard's economic concept.

Bundestag Election Results (splinter parties omitted); in percentages:

	1949	1953	1957	1961
CDU/CSU (Christian Democrats)	31.0	45.2	50.2	45.3
SPD (Social Democrats)	29.2	28.8	31.8	36.2
FDP (Free Democrats, Liberals)	11.9	9.5	7.7	12.8

29. See, e.g., the paper read by the director of *Deutsche Industrieinstitut,* published *Vortragsreihe des D.I.,* Jg. 14, Nr. 4, Jan. 28, 1964: "If competition were removed or restricted, then, in the long run, a point would be inescapably reached where political and economic freedom would be nothing but empty words."

30. See for example K. Albrecht (secretary general of Chamber of Commerce at Düsseldorf), *Planifikateure beim Werk, Wirtschaftzwischen Zwang und Freiheit* (Düsseldorf, 1964); a very critical report on French, Dutch, and European "programing" and "planification." See also the very instructive report of the *List Gesellschaft* on its convention on planning, published by A. Plitzko under the title *Planung ohne Planwirtschaft* (Basel and Tübingen, 1964). Recently *Planung in der Marktwirtschaft,* proceedings of a convention organized by Friedrich Naumann Foundation (Stuttgart, 1964).

31. The book on economic policy written by the head of the Freiburg school, Eucken, was published after his death. Its technical part is very noncommittal.

32. For instance H. von Stackelberg, *"Möglichkeiten und Grenzen der*

Wirtschaftslenkung," *ORDO,* Bd. 2 (Bad Godesberg, 1949), p. 203. "Far-reaching interventions into income distribution are possible without the market system as such being abolished." See also L. Miksch, *Die Geldschöpfung in der Gleichgewichtstheorie, ORDO, ibid.,* p. 327.

33. This claim for "universality" (*Allgemeinheit*) of law is another basic prerequisite of neoliberalism. See for instance Hayek, who in this respect is representative of the Freiburg school and its policy: "Government must limit itself to 'general rules of law' instead of issuing administrative decisions which are based on pragmatic utility and, therefore, on discretion; the special orders or prohibitions directed to particular persons, which cannot be anticipated by their very nature. . . . Functioning of the market system demands that uncertainty which can be avoided should be reduced to a minimum. Therefore, the State must limit itself by general rules, and not command the aims of the economy itself, so that the individual economic subjects can utilize the state machinery according to their purposes. This, to witness, is the essence of a free economic system (*das Wesen der freien Wirtschaftsordnung*)," Hayek, *Marktwirtschaft und Wirtschaftspolitik,* in *ORDO,* Bd. 6 (Bad Godesberg, 1954), p. 9. Hayek adds himself, that this could be "pure theory"; but in another volume of *ORDO,* his book *The Road to Serfdom* is enthusiastically reviewed by the vice president of a German Central Bank affiliate, Irmler, in *ORDO,* Bd. 2 (Bad Godesberg, 1949), p. 339.

34. Jan. 7, 1952, *Investitionshilfegesetz* (*BGBl.* I, 7).

35. See the expert opinion of Forsthoff, mentioned in E. R. Huber, *Wirtschaftsverwaltungsrecht,* Bd. II (Tübingen, 1954), p. 230.

36. *Umsiedlungsverordnung,* Nov. 29, 1949, *BGBl.* 1950, Nr. 2, p. 4. *Bundesvertriebenengesetz,* May 22, 1951, *BGBl.* I, p. 350, revised May 19, 1953, *BGBl.* 1953, I, Nr. 22, p. 201.

37. *Soforthilfegesetz,* August 8, 1949, Wi GBl. 1949, Nr. 28, p. 205. *Lastenausgleichsgesetz,* August 14, 1952, *BGBl.* I, p. 446.

38. Sept. 18, 1953, *Bundesergänzungsgesetz zur Entschädigung für Opfer der nationalsozialistischen Verfolgung, BGBl,* I, 1387. June 29, 1956, *Bundesentschädingungsgesetz, BGBl,* I, 550.

39. Apr. 24, 1950, 1. *Wohnungsbaugesetz, BGBl.* I, 83. June 28, 1956, 2. *Wohnungsbaugesetz, BGBl.* I, 523.

40. Sept. 15, 1953, *Einkommensteuerergänzung,* introduction of Par. 7c into Income Tax Law (for revised version of Aug. 15, 1961 see *BGBl.* I, p. 1254). March 31, 1953, *Wohnraumbewirtschaftungsgesetz, BGBl.* I, Nr. 14, p. 97.

41. Sources: 1) *Statistisches Jahrbuch der Bundesrepublik;* 2) *Bericht über das Ergebnis einer Untersuchung der Konzentration in der Wirtschaft,* February 29, 1964, *Bundestag-Drucksache* IV/2320, 4. *Wahlperiode,* p. 48.

42. See Erhard, *op. cit.,* p. 29.

43. *Kindergeldgesetz* of Nov. 13, 1954, *BGBl.* I, 333.

44. Such as *Wohnungsbauprämiengesetz* of Mar. 17, 1952, *BGBl.* I, Nr. 10, p. 139; since Jan. 1, 1955, many forms of savings can be made tax

exempt; for an instance of "investment wage" see *Gesetz zur Förderung der Vermögensbildung der Arbeitnehmer* of July 12, 1961, *BGBl.* I, 909. All these measures were meant to set into effect the so-called "second phase of *Soziale Marktwirtschaft*," namely the increase of private capital holdings by a broader mass of people. Since the increase in saving is achieved by subsidies, some argue that this policy has a negative effect: it denatures saving as well as capital. The Experts' Council of the Ministry of Finance has recently voted against continuation of these subsidies for saving.

45. *Bergarbeiterwohnungsabgabe* of Oct. 30, 1951, *BGBl.* I, Nr. 51, p. 879. Subsidizing of *Knappschaftsversicherung,* contained as *Einzelplan* 11, *Kapitel* 13, *Titel* 602, in annual federal budget.

46. *Aenderung des Grundsteuergesetzes im Bundesbaugesetz* of June 12, 1960, *BGBl.* I, 341, sec. 172, concerning alteration of Real Estate Tax Law, Einfügung der sec. 12 a, b, c.

47. Discrimination can be based on par. 23, *Aussenwirtschaftsgesetz,* of Apr. 28, 1961, *BGBl.* I, Nr. 29, p. 481, Nr. 69, p. 1555.

48. *Subventionen im Bundeshaushalt, Drucksache* 1229, of July 28, 1959, 3. The federal budget amounted, in 1959, to 39.8 billion marks.

49. Landwirtschaftsgesetz of Sept. 5, 1955, *BGBl.* I, p. 565, sec. 4.

50. Reichsgesetz über das Kreditwesen, of Dec. 5, 1934, *BGBl.* I, 1456; revised by new Kreditwesengesetz, of July 10, 1961, *BGBl.* 1961, I, Nr. 49, p. 881.

51. Mitbestimmungsgesetz, of May 21, 1951, *BGBl.* I, p. 347.

52. For a preliminary appraisal see H. Popitz *et al., Das Gesellschaftsbild des Arbeiters* (Tübingen, 1957); and Fritz Voigt and Walter Weddingen, *Zur Theorie und Praxis der Mitbestimmung* (Berlin, 1962).

53. *Betriebsverfassungsgesetz* of October 11, 1952, *BGBl.* I, p. 681.

54. *Gesetz über den Ladenschluss* of Nov. 28, 1956, *BGBl.* I, Nr. 50, p. 875.

55. See *Erster Bericht der Bundesregierung über die Raumordnung,* of Oct. 1, 1963; 4. Bundestag Drucksache IV/1492. See Chapter V for details.

56. Rentenversicherungs-Neuordnungsgesetz, *RGBl.* I, 4/1957, 45.

57. Baustop-Gesetz of June 8, 1962, *BGBl.* I, p. 365.

58. Quoted in note 41 above.

59. *Erklärung des Bundeskanzlers* (Professor Erhard) of Oct. 18, 1963, 90. *Sitzung, 4. Wahlperiode.* In June, 1964, a committee was called to start an Inquiry into Social Interrelations (*Sozialenquête,* published in 1966).

60. For this, see A. Rüstow, "Die staatspolitischen Voraussetzungen des wirtschaftspolitischen Liberalismus," *Der Deutsche Volkswirt,* Jg. 7, Nr. 6 (Berlin, 1932), p. 169.

61. According to registration office of the federal parliament, to that must be added the 2968 decrees passed during the same period (registered from first to third session of the Bundestag).

62. Baustop-Gesetz, see note 57 above.

63. Grundsteuer C, see note 46 above.

64. See note 74 below.

65. Ministries for Food, Economics, Labor, and other specialized economic administrations were not introduced until World War I, in most cases not until 1949.

66. As an example we may mention the embargo for pipes and tubes exported to the Soviet bloc which unexpectedly was decreed in Dec., 1962. The embargo was maintained against the solid pressure of both industry and specialized ministries and finally backed up by a parliamentary vote in 1963 during the 68th Session, 4. Wahlperiode, Drucksache IV/858, 1071.

67. Here we have to point to the much debated privileges of interlocking corporations which allegedly are meant to avoid double taxation in corporation and/or turnover tax, but which discriminate against smaller enterprises (*Organgesellschaft, Umsatzsteuergesetz* of Oct. 16, 1934, *RGBl.* I, 942, Par. 2, 2, 2; *Schachtelprivileg, Körperschaftssteuergesetz* of Sept. 13, 1961, *BGBl.* I, 1722, par. 9). Privileges of this sort are again and again demanded; see *"Steuererleichterung für Stahlwerke,"* in *Die Welt,* Jan. 4, 1964.

68. It is here that demands for "rationalizing economic policy" (see Chap. VI) and for macroeconomic accounting converge. For comparing national accounting measures of several governments, see the publication of *Forschungsstelle der Friedrich-Ebert-Stiftung, Nationalbudget und Wirtschaftspolitik* (Hanover, 1962).

69. For this, see for instance A. Gehlen, *"Soziologische Aspekte des Eigentumsproblems in der Industrie-Gesellschaft,"* Eigentum und Eigentümer, Veröffentlichungen der Walter-Raymond-Stiftung* (Foundation of Management Associations) (Cologne and Opladen, 1960), p. 183.

70. See, for instance, note 30 to this chapter and *Langfristige Programmierung innerhalb der Marktwirtschaft,* Report on part of the 26th Convention of *Arbeitsgemeinschaft deutscher wirtschaftswissenschaftlicher Forschungsinstitute,* June 21 and 22, 1963 (Berlin, 1963), published as *Beiheft no. 10 der Konjunkturpolitik.* A recent publication is *Planung I,* J. H. Kaiser, ed. (Baden-Baden, 1966).

71. For this Act see note 58, Chap. V.

72. See Chap. V.

73. There was an open clash between the president of the Central Bank and Federal Chancellor Adenauer concerning restrictive measures in May, 1956. See Meimberg, *Einige Grundfagen . . . , op. cit.,* pp. 238–39.

74. See Bundestag vote on special tariff reduction for automobiles on June 25, 1962, *BGBl.* II, p. 839.

75. To prepare this finance reform, another expert committee has been instituted by the Federal Chancellor and the prime ministers of the Länder. The Social Democrats—represented in this body by their Länder governments—claim that the committee should take a position also on long-term economic programing in connection with fiscal reform (see *"Langfristige Vorausschau gehört zum Programm,"* in *Die Welt,* March 23, 1964).

76. For details see Chap. V.

III. The "Social Market" Model

1. W. Eucken, *Grundsätze der Wirtschaftspolitik* (Hamburg, 1959), pp. 34, 54.

2. *Ibid.*, p. 94.

3. *Ibid.*, pp. 99–109.

4. *Ibid.*, pp. 160–61.

5. *Ibid.*, n. 2, p. 163.

6. *Ibid.*, p. 162.

7. See Müller-Armack, *Wirtschaftslenkung und Marktwirtschaft*, p. 19.

8. Eucken, *op. cit.*, p. 183.

9. *Ibid.*, pp. 188–89.

10. Von Stackelberg, *Möglichkeiten und Grenzen*, p. 203; Miksch, *Die Geldschöpfung in der Gleichgewichtstheorie*, p. 327.

11. Eucken, *op. cit.*, pp. 187, 182.

12. See note 17, Chap. II.

13. On Oct. 29, 1963, the federal minister of economics published a *Primer on Cooperation* (I B 5—81 33 50) in an attempt to help small businesses to find legal ways for cooperating in spite of existing law. This primer has been openly criticized because of its undesirable results.

14. See, for instance, the Report on the Convention of *Verein für Sozialpolitik 1960, Die Konzentration in der Wirtschaft* (Berlin, 1961), especially the contribution of E. Salin, as a sharp advocate of concentration.

15. Popitz *et al., op. cit.*, found that 75 per cent of the workers of a sample wanted to work in big industry (p. 91). An interest of the late Professor Röpke, chief designer of neoliberalism and mentor of Erhard, the Swiss economy sometimes is said to be the model of the Freiburg school, and it is sometimes attacked for not taking modern bigness into consideration.

16. See, e.g., the editor's introduction to *Planung ohne Planwirtschaft*.

17. Decision of the Federal Constitutional Court of Aug. 17, 1956, outlawing the German Communist party. The decision was based on Art. 21, sec. 2, of the Basic law (Constitution) of the Federal Republic.

18. *"Nivellierte Mitelstandsgesellschaft"*: H. Schelsky, ed., *et al., Arbeiterjugend gestern und heute* (Heidelberg, 1955); E. Zahn, *Sociologie der Prosperität* (Cologne and Berlin, 1960).

19. See O. Kirchheimer, *"Vom Wandel der politischen Opposition," Archiv für Rechts- und Sozialphilosophie* (1957), XLIII/1.

20. Karl Schiller, leading economic expert of the Social Democrats, published a booklet *Sozialismus und Wettbewerb* (Hamburg, 1955) as a professor, not as Berlin Senator which he later became; the annual forum of the Central Association of German Labor Unions (*Deutscher Gewerkschaftsbund*) of 1961 for three days discussed the problem *"Sachverstand und Politik in der Demokratie"* (ed. under this title Düsseldorf, 1962), meaning "experts and politicians in a democracy." See also G. Leibholz, "Der Einfluss der Fachleute auf politische Entscheidungen," in *Die politische Verantwortung der Nichtpolitiker* (Munich, 1965).

141

21. That "classical" government has macroeconomic functions is not yet universally accepted in West Germany; "the State" is still viewed with the eyes of a skeptical liberalist as a (fiscal) micro-entity, see e.g.: "The economics without a subject is called today macroeconomics; economic actions of individual subjects is microeconomics. The economy of government (*Staatswirtschaft*) and the public budget belong to the latter sphere, because here we have to do with economic action of a subject" (F. von Dungern, *"Die drei Theorien vom Staatshaushalt," Zeitschrift für die gesamte Staatswissenschaft*, Bd. 108 (1952), p. 460; and L. von Mises, *Theorie des Geldes und der Umlaufsmittel* (Munich and Leipzig, 1912), p. 56—still considered valid: "The function of the State in the market is in no way different from that of any other subject participating in market transactions."

22. *Industrielle Massengesellschaft* (industrialized mass society)—another term much used—probably in order to avoid emotionally loaded older sociologisms (see e.g., A. Gehlen, *Die Seele im technischen Zeitalter* [Hamburg, 1947]).

23. See e.g., B. de Jouvenel, *De la Souveraineté, à la recherche du bien politique* (Paris, 1955), p. 170: "Whoever claims to execute what he calls the global interest of the whole is a dangerous fool." By "economic whole" must be understood here the mass of interrelations, the matrix consisting of individual actions; not potential targets of the entire process (such as harmonious growth, stable money, or full employment). Political regulation of these targets is acknowledged as compatible with the system of neoliberalists.

24. On *Massnahmegesetz*, see E. Forsthoff, *Lehrbuch des Verwaltungsrechts*, 7th ed. (Munich and Berlin, 1958), pp. 9, 119–20, 184. Same author: *Über Massnahmegesetze, in Forschungen und Berichte aus dem öffentlichen Recht, Jellinek-Gedächtnisschrift* (Munich, 1955). The same author has used the term *"Daseinsvorsorge"* as a concept of administrative law.

25. The so-called *"Masshalte-Appelle"* of Erhard are, in a sense, contrary to market principles. If the market will pay, why not take?

26. One of the first ones to speak of a particular brand of "pluralistic society" in West Germany was W. Weber, *Spannungen und Kräfte im westdeutschen Verfassungssystem* (Stuttgart, 1951).

27. Notable is the struggle on the question whether the currency shall be revalued or not, which comes up again and again and engages all interest groups according to the export-import position, all groups claiming to argue in the common interest.

28. For instance by J. Habermas, *Strukturwandel der Oeffentlichkeit* (Neuwied, 1962), p. 218, following R. A. Dahl, "Hierarchy, Democracy, and Bargaining in Politics and Economics," in *Research Frontiers in Politics and Government* (Washington, D.C., 1955).

29. In this context have to be viewed the various attempts to find a solution for the perplexing problem of party financing. Art. 21, sec. 3 of Basic Law (Constitution) stipulated in 1949 that a law on these issues had to be made. In 1957, a report was published by a Committee named by the federal minister of the interior (*Rechtliche Ordnung des Parteiwesens* [Frank-

furt/M., 1957]). Legislative action has not yet been taken, but there are two Supreme Court decisions and many proposals of which some openly admit the full commercialization of parties (and even votes).

30. Reminiscent of a statement of O. Morgenstern (*Die Grenzen der Wirtschaftspolitik* [Vienna, 1934], S. V): "An absolutist-autocratic government not only does not contradict a liberalist economic policy, but, to the contrary, it gives it a much greater chance—once it has been decided. The reason is that a liberal economic order does not so much require specific positive actions, as the refusal to act. An authoritarian state can really say 'no.' "

31. A formulation used by the FDP (Liberal party) M.P., Th. Dehler, later vice-president of Parliament, to denounce all specific measures, especially tax exemptions.

32. The addressee was the president of a pressure group organized to support Erhard's neoliberalist concept, the *Aktionsgemeinschaft Soziale Marktwirtschaft*. The secretary of state was an "expert," not a party man.

IV. Men and Their Motives: The Sociological Scene

1. Colin Clark, *The Conditions of Economic Progress*, 3rd ed. (London, 1957). See for illustration the structural statistics in Appendix.

2. This usage occurs in A. Schumpeter's famous book, *Theorie der wirtschaftlichen Entwicklung* (Munich, 1913).

3. For this view see, e.g., G. N. Halm, *Geld, Aussenhandel und Beschäftigung*, 3rd ed., translated (Munich, 1957), p. 275; and L. Gleske, *Die Liquidität in der Kreditwirtschaft* (Frankfurt/M., 1953), p. 7.

4. Cf. the ASU periodical *Die Aussprache*, published in Bad Godesburg.

5. See note 44, Chap. II.

6. See D. Granick, *The European Executive* (New York, 1962), Chap. 4: "Germany: Manager vs. Entrepreneur," *passim*. The *Institut für Demoskopie* at Allensback (opinion polls) has conducted regular polls on the public image of the entrepreneur, which may be used for a comprehensive study.

7. This is a junior circle within the ASU; there are also junior circles of Chambers of Commerce, etc.

8. Here we are following David Riesman *et al.*, *The Lonely Crowd* (New Haven), 1950).

9. Among the generation just described as "sons," one may find a very able managing executive who pushes into the open air of "independent" entrepreneurship (some of them have gone bankrupt again in the meantime); but on the average what has been left of the son generation by the war behaves cautiously to the point of shunning risk and authority.

10. See Granick, *op. cit.*, p. 61.

11. Cf. W. Zangen (former president of the board of Mannesmann), *Die Praxis der industriellen Unternehmensführung*, 2nd ed. (Essen, 1962), p. 20: "Entrepreneurial action is not primarily determined by a property

status. . . . True competence for being an entrepreneur will show in critical times. . . . In those times it will be possible to ascertain without bias who has the nature of an entrepreneur [*Unternehmernatur*], and who has not."

12. See, e.g., *ibid.*: "This group of persons (managers) not only pays (*haftet*) with their good name, in the last instance, but also with their entire fortune, for actions which damage the enterprise."

13. See for instance the wide range of views on this subject expressed by the various participants of the Conference on planning, reproduced in *Planung ohne Planwirtschaft*, especially on June 8, 1963.

14. It is not by chance that a leading French "technocrat" who endorses planning is, at the same time, a champion of the restriction of property rights and of a change in the "constitution" of the enterprise, which comes very close to a universal application of decisive parts of German "Co-Determination." See F. Bloch-Lainé, *Pour une réforme de l'entreprise* (Paris, 1963). This book is also debated in West Germany..

15. See sources cited in notes 51 and 53, Chap. II.

16. Open, but not used. The figures for high school and university attendance still show a marked disequilibrium towards "hereditary" education in West Germany.

17. This cry for "generalization" or "universalism" of management trainees seems to us to be indicative of the fact that private property has changed its role. Formerly it was the property holders who introduced the "universalist" outlook into business; most of their leading hired personnel could be specialized. Nowadays, owners do not differ from creditors; hence top management has to despecialize in order to reach a degree of universal responsibility which, in former times, could be found only with house mayors of families or—in rare instances—self-made autocrats of stockholding companies with wide share distribution.

18. For instance, the Mannesmann Board President Zangen (quoted in note 11 above) was called to this office in 1934, retired to Supervisory Council in 1957.

19. See Granick, *op. cit.*, Chap. 21: "Germany: Early Selection of Oligarchs."

20. These centers are informally organized by the so-called "Wuppertaler Kreis," the secretariat of which (*Deutsches Institut zur Förderung des industriellen Führungsnachwuchses*) publishes a calendar listing all management courses in West Germany. There is international cooperation.

21. For a critique of this activity, see Th. Eschenburg, *Herrschaft der Verbände* (Stuttgart, 1955); an extensive report gives R. Breitling, *Die Verbände in der Bundesrepublik* (Meisenheim/Glan, 1955).

22. For instance: private banking badly lacked skilled people, when, in 1958, "buying on the margin" of foreign exchange was allowed for the first time since 1931. It was the same with lockout, many entrepreneurs and managers of the younger generation felt not quite sure about the technicalities when facing the lockout in 1963. The general strike—a "political strike"—as proclaimed and won in 1920 against the plot of rightist generals and

officials under von Lüttwitz and Kapp is usually cited as the best example of this function of "watchdog and avant-garde of human rights and democracy."

23. This change towards pragmatism was urgently required in order to build up union membership. It is a tough job to maintain membership relative to the working force, as has been done in West Germany, with the high degree of fluctuation between industries and, hence, unions. To tackle technical obstacles, the unions had to remove ideological barriers to compete for membership.

24. *Entwurf eines Gesetzes zur Ergänzung des Tarifvertragsgesetzes* of October 29, 1957, Drucksache 8, 3. Bundestag.

25. Cf. *Wirtschaftswissenschaftliches Institut des Deutschen Gewerkschaftsbundes, Notenbank im Umbau* (Cologne, 1951); *Bundesgenossen der Bundesbankunabhängigkeit, in Zeitschrift für das gesamte Kreditwesen* (1951), p. 386.

26. See C. J. Friedrich, "The Continental Tradition of Training Administrators in Law and Jurisprudence," *Journal of Modern History*, Vol. XI, No. 2 (1939).

27. An interesting sidelight: The former head of the German Supreme Constitutional Court (*Bundesverfassungsgericht*) confessed in 1953, in an interview, that he was at heart a monarchist (*Der Spiegel*, February 11, 1953, interview with President Hoepker-Aschoff).

28. See Eschenburg citation in note 21 above.

29. See Chap. V for details.

30. For the open clash between Erhard and Hallstein, see Chap. V.

31. Source: *Der 17. September unter der Lupe, Deutsches Industrie-Institut* (Cologne, 1961), *aus der Schriftenreihe: Material zum Zeitgeschehen*, Nr. 10, 1961. Another source utilized for further data, H.-E. Jahn, *Gesellschaft und Demokratie in der Zeitwende*, 2nd ed. (Cologne, 1955), p. 169.

32. See Introduction to H. von Mangoldt, *Das Bonner Grundgesetz* (Berlin and Frankfurt, 1953).

33. It is here that the so-called "predominance of the executive branch" enters in; in other words, the role of the government bureaucracy which is—as was just explained—trained in jurisprudence.

34. See R. T. McKenzie, *British Political Parties* (Melbourne, London, and Toronto, 1955). According to West German electorate laws, one-half of the M.P.'s are elected by proportionate representation, one-half by direct vote; but the mass of representatives is calculated on a proportionate basis.

35. On the importance of committee work in Bonn, see B. Dechamps, *Macht und Arbeit der Ausschüsse* (Meisenheim/Glan, 1954).

36. G. Schmölders, *Die Politiker und die Währung.* (Report on a demoscopic study of public opinion on financial and currency questions, conducted among members of the third Bundestag) (Frankfurt/M., 1959).

37. Abgeordneter Schmücker, 48. Sitzung, 2. Bundestag, Oct. 14, 1954, Protocol S. 2342A.

38. So-called "Lex Münnemann" of May 25, 1959, contained as par. 12, sec. 3, of *Kapitalverkehrssteuergesets* (revised version *BGBl.* I, 530, of July 24, 1959).

V. Groups and Their Policies

1. The RKW was founded—with a slightly different name—in 1921. Today it has about 1,500 members, among the central associations of business, labor, science, technology and government. Its work is purely consultative. The 1962 Congress was explicitly devoted to planning.

2. See note 3, Chap. III, on the effect of the government's *Cooperation Primer*.

3. See works cited in note 30, Chap. II.

4. A. Plitzko, *Planung ohne Planwirtschaft*, p. 93.

5. The West German Cartel Board (Kartellamt) is gradually following along; on Aug. 14, 1963, it published "administrative principles" (*Verwaltungsgrundsätze*) bearing on the organization of specialization cartels (see *Die Welt*, Aug. 15, 1963).

6. See Plitzko, *op. cit.*, p. 93.

7. *Ibid.*, p. 95.

8. *Ibid.*

9. *Ibid.*

10. As an early example see Jeidels, *Das Verhältnis der Grossbanken zur Industrie* (Leipzig, 1905). For details of the present see the *Report on the Result of an Inquiry into the Concentration of the Economy*, part B, sect. 3, p. 35.

11. See *Report on Concentration . . .*, pp. 35–36.

12. For instance, the municipal savings banks organized themselves on a nationwide scale in order to profit from the balancing of cash flow inside the organization (*Girozentralen*). The Concentration Inquiry (p. 43) gives the following figures on the importance of the three giant banks (Deutsche, Dresdner, and Commerzbank):

Subject	Per cent Held by Giant Banks
Participation in 343 reported banks	50
Participation of 343 banks in other business	66
Number of seats in Supervising Boards held by banks	52
Number of votes represented by banks in shareholders' conventions	70
Money value of bonds issued by all business	66
Clients deposited in 343 reported banks:	
shares	55
fixed-interest obligations and bonds	34
investment shares	58

13. For instance, coal mines are organized into a "Rationalization Association" which pays premium sums for mining corporations which close down an unprofitable pit. Incidentally, this example is spreading: the cotton

industry wants, in 1964, to follow suit (see *Der Spiegel,* Nr. 28, July 8, 1964).

1960, five pits producing (in 1957) 2,4 mio.t of coal were closed
1961, four pits producing (in 1957) 1,6 mio.t of coal were closed
1962, seven pits producing (in 1957) 3,4 mio.t of coal were closed

14. See works cited in note 25, Chap. IV above.

15. *Die Welt,* March 21, 1964.

16. See *Grundsatzprogramm des Deutschen Gewerkschaftsbundes,* Resolved at the Extraordinary Federal Congress of DGB on Nov. 21 and 22, 1963.

17. These and other quotes are from the program cited above. For the Social Democrats, see K. Schiller, *Sozialismus und Wettbewerb.*

18. The Constitution of the Land Hessen of Dec. 1, 1946 (Art. 41) prescribes the nationalization of mining, iron and steel production, energy, and traffic fixed to rails or wires. It is noteworthy that the Constitution of the Federal Republic (Grundgesetz), designed much later (in 1948–49), also contains Art. 15, which allows for nationalization and transformation into "Gemeinwirtschaft." A group of M.P.'s has used a bill introduced in the Bundestag for abrogation of this article to embarrass the Christian Democrats (*Entwurf eines Gesetzes zur Änderung des Artikels 15 des Grundgesetzes* of Nov. 4, 1957, Drucksache 1336).

19. *Bundesvereinigung der Deutschen Arbeitgeberverbände, Stellungnahme zum DBG-Grundsatzprogram* (Cologne, 1963). See also note 16 above.

20. All quotes from this *Stellungnahme,* pp. 6, 7.

21. It is not accidental that the Central Association of Labor (DGB) conducted its 12th (annual) "European Convention," held in 1963, on the topic "The autonomy of the trade unions in an integrated Europe" (*Die Autonomie der Gewerkschaften in einem integrierten Europa* [Düsseldorf, 1964]).

22. Art. 9 Basic Law guarantees the right to strike and to lockout.

23. See D. Hiss, *Kosten und Preise in der Bundesrepublik bis 1960* (Berlin, 1963).

24. See note 56, Chap. II.

25. The author quoted in note 23 above claims (p. 46) that linking nominal wages to productivity increases does not even protect management against a changed income distribution favoring labor.

26. The Act is quoted later.

27. In some Länder there exists an office for voluntary arbitration of labor disputes. Its task may be inferred from the title of an article published in *Die Welt,* Dec. 15, 1962: "Fire department, midwife, and catalyst—the Land arbitrator of North Rhine Westphalia." The article was written in order to prove that "a law on voluntary arbitration is unnecessary."

28. "Fürst lehnt Vorsitz ab," in *Die Welt,* March 29, 1962.

29. Wage contracts are nowadays sometimes concluded for one year and

NOTES

147

a half. This is not a "guaranteed annual wage"; it is not the pay but its "how and how much" which are guaranteed.

30. This amounts to a sort of "minimum clause" to which agreements of (private) partners are made by government decree, thus effecting something which is rather peculiar in jurisprudence, namely binding third parties by contracts of two other parties. The "Declaration of Universal Validity" (Allgemeinverbindlichkeitserklärung) can be rather delicate for government when it concerns a contract entering a *terra nova*, such as the Contract of the Construction Industry. Applications for Declaration of Universal Validity must be directed to the Ministries of Labor (of Federation or Länder), where a committee composed of management and labor helps to decide the issue.

31. Article 21 of Basic Law, German Federal Republic.

32. For this, see R. Altmann, *"Zur Rechtsstellung der öffentlichen Verbände," Zeitschrift für Politik,* Bd. II (1955), p. 214. The DGB (Federation of Labor Unions) has not even taken the trouble of registering in the official register for private societies.

33. For instance, the Federation of German Industries (BdI)—or at least its official mouthpiece—had a less dogmatically negative attitude towards macroeconomic programing. This was expressed on the occasion of the public debate about long-term programing as proposed by the Brussels authorities. The BdI demanded "an especially intensive scrutinizing" of the plans; "in no case can there be an interference with the freedom of action *(Dispositionsfreiheit)* of the enterprises" *(Die Welt,* Nov. 24, 1962). For a recent statement of the institute controlled by BdI, see: *Prognosen als Grundlage der Wirtschaftspolitik, Beiträge des Deutschen Industrie-Instituts,* No. 1 (1964). This publication shows a somewhat more cautious attitude towards long-term programing. Other associations, e.g., sub-groups of the BdI, are also in the process of forming their opinion. See, e.g., the periodical Chemische Industrie (ed. by the Association of Chemical Industries, Heft 5 [1963]: H. Meinhold, *Aspekte einer europäischen Programmierung).*

34. Altmann, *op. cit.,* p. 216.

35. Habermas, *Strukturwandel der Oeffentlichkeit,* p. 219.

36. *Ibid.*

37. The Coal Miners' Union leader protested in 1959 against a reduction of employment in the mines (which could be proved necessary for rationalization reasons) with the words: "You don't beg for an existential right *(ein Lebensrecht),* you fight for it" *(Die Welt,* Jan. 26, 1959): he meant by "existential right" the right to earn money in the pits (into which many miners had gone some years ago without any "existential reflection," and which they would like to quit when they found other places to earn better money).

38. *Die Welt,* June 30, 1964.

39. Cf. H. Schelsky, *Einsamkeit und Freiheit, Idee und Gestalt der deutschen Universität und ihrer Reformen* (Hamburg, 1963), *Rowohlts Deutsche Enzyklop.*

40. For an opponent of Max Weber see, e.g., his brother Alfred Weber, *Prinzipien der Geschichts- und Kultursoziologie* (Munich, 1951).

41. Art. 110 and 113, Bonn Basic Law, supported by Par. 20, *Bundesbankgesetz,* which sets limits for credits of the Central Bank to all public administration treasuries.

42. For an example, see H. Fischer (member of the board, Brose Advertising & Marketing Co.), *Marketing* (Stuttgart, 1959).

43. Such banks were used to execute the Lastenausgleich Program, Expellee Acts, or Investment Aid Act; it is rather bold to classify them as "commercial banks."

44. Figures quoted from Concentration Inquiry (see note 41, Chap. II).

45. As an example, see *Gesetz über die wirtschaftliche Betätigung der öffentlichen Hand,* Drucksache 2712, 2. Bundestag, which tried to legislate compulsory re-privatization of all government property which could be commercialized. The bill was not accepted (introduced by Liberal party); later followed the denationalization of single firms (see above notes 19 and 21, Chap. II).

46. The Volkswagen company, e.g., did not sell all its shares. The Federal Administration and the government of Land Niedersachsen (where the main plants are located) kept a substantial bloc by employment of a foundation system. The Land government, incidentally, has often been Socialist.

47. See note 74, Chap. II above.

48. See for instance *Annalen der Gemeinwirtschaft* (Annals of Collective Economy), *Die Organisation der Wirtschaft im Dienste des Menschen,* Report on the VIth International Convention of Collective Economy in Apr., 1963, Heft 2/3, 32, Jahrgang (April-September, 1963). Most of the German members of this Convention were Social Democrats.

49. See Arndt, *Politik und Sachverstand im Kreditwahrungswesen* (Berlin, 1963).

50. This had been observed as early as 1912 (see J. Plenge, *Von der Diskontpolitik zur Herrschaft über den Geldmarkt* [Berlin, 1913], p. 354).

51. See Article 3 of *Bundesbankgesetz* (*Gesetz über die Deutsche Bundesbank* of July 26, 1957, *BGBl.* I, 745).

52. See Meimberg, *Einige Grundfragen . . . ,* pp. 238–39.

53. *Gesetz über die Statistik für Bundeszwecke* of Sept. 3, 1953, *BGBl.* I, 1314.

54. *Die Welt,* March 29, 1962.

55. See *Die Welt,* July 2, 1964.

56. Rentenversicherungs-Neuordnungsgesetz, *RGBl.* 1, 4/1957, 45.

57. See Chap. II and Chap. II above; *Die Welt,* June 29, 1964.

58. *Gesetz über die Einrichtung eines Sachverständigenrates für gesamtwirtschaftliche Entwicklung* of Aug. 14, 1963, *BGBl.* I, 685.

59. See *Die Welt,* Jan. 20, 1964.

60. The publication of the 12th Annual Convention of the Central Federation of German Labor (DGB), *Die Autonomie der Gewerkschaften in einem integrierten Europa* closes with a list of all European "Joint Labor-Management Councils" (*Die wichtigsten Merkmale der überbetrieblichen*

Räte in Europa, p. 319). Recently the Expert Council of the Ministry of Economics published a negative opinion concerning the re-establishment of a Federal Economic Council (*Bundeswirtschaftsrat*). Instead, greater publicity for lobbying was recommended (*Die Welt,* July 23, 1964). Some Länder Constitutions have created *"Wirtschaftsräte,"* which have little effect.

61. *Die Welt,* Nov. 19, 1962.

62. See note 31 above.

63. The problem is complex. For example, in the case of the embargo on tubes, the secretary-general of the association representing the steel industry, an M.P., observed party discipline and voted for the embargo, although he had argued on behalf of his association against it (for the vote see note 66, Chap. II). Former minister, later president, of the Management Association Balke voted, in the fall of 1963, aganst an SPD motion to create an expert council for health insurance. In the spring of 1964, he launched the same proposal in his role as management president (See the article "Balke," *Die Welt,* April, 1964).

64. On the Land level, such proposals have been made in election campaigns, e.g. in North Rhine-Westphalia by the later Minister W. Weyer, during the campaign of 1957. They had no practical effect.

65. Source: *Finanzbericht of 1964,* Ministry of Finance: GNP in 1962 was: 355 billion marks. Estimated Growth Rate in 1963 was a nominal 6 per cent.

66. The proportion of total tax receipts, in percentage of GNP, is said to have risen from 21.7 to 24.2 during the last five years, according to a pronouncement of the federal minister of finance (*Die Welt,* May 30, 1964).

67. According to the Hamburg senator for finance, even 90 per cent to 95 per cent (*Die Welt, ibid.*).

68. This is the argument used, e.g., by G. Strickrodt, *Die Finanzordnung als Lebensbasis der arbeitsteiligen Wirtschaft, Vortrag, Karlsruher Versicherungswoche,* April 29, 1955.

69. For instance in *Die Welt,* Dec. 21, 1962.

70. Hamburg Senator Weichmann, in *Die Welt,* May 30, 1964.

71. *Bundesjugendplan,* contained as *Einzelplan 29, Titel 571,* in annual federal budget.

72. For the Act see Chap. II.

73. For this and the following statistics, see L. Blum, *"Der Grüne Bericht 1964," Die Aussparche,* ed. *Arbeitsgemeinschaft selbständiger Unternehmer,* March 3, 1964.

74. There are 572,000 "Full Farming Units" (*Vollbauernstellen*) among the 1.76 million units which are statistically reported (and receivers of farm aid) according to the Federal Statistical Office (*Die Welt,* Jan. 4, 1964).

75. Drucksache IV, 1492, Deutscher Bundestag, 4. Wahlperiode. Answer to the Resolution of Deutscher Bundestag of Feb. 15 and March 6, 1963, Drucksache IV, 473.

76. See the reaction of the Stuttgart Mayor Klett, *Die Welt,* June 1, 1964.

77. See *Die Welt,* March 25, 1963.

78. See source cited in note 20, Chap. II, and *Die Welt,* April 7, 1964.

79. *Vereinigung der Deutschen Staatsrechtslehrer, Der Plan als verwaltungsrechtliches Institut. Veröffentlichungen* Heft 18 (Berlin, 1960).
80. *Die Welt,* June 13, 1964. See new Bill on Stabilization, introduced in 1966.
81. Drucksache IV, 1752, of Dec. 11, 1963, Deutscher Bundestag, 4. Wahlperiode, and *zu* Drucksache IV, 1752, of June 8, 1964.
82. The Bundesrat is the second federal Chamber, representing the Länder.
83. Report, English trans., p. 3.
84. Annexed to the Report are seven tables of statistics showing figures of National Accounts as follows: Gainful Activity; Contributions by Sectors to the Gross Domestic Product at Market Prices; Distribution of the National Income; Wage and Salary Incomes; Incomes from Entrepreneurial Activity and Property; Incomes and Consumption; and Appropriation of the National Product.
85. See Erhard, *Wohlstand für Alle,* p. 24.
86. For these special banks see above.
87. OEEC, *Europas Energie-Bedarf, sein Anwachsen, seine Deckung, Bericht einer Sachverstaendigengruppe,* ed. *Bundesministerium für wirtschaftliche Zusammenarbeit* (Bonn, 1956).
88. It had to move on to a new phase in agricultural policy according to a deadline which was prescribed by law, in 1962–63.
89. *Die Welt,* Nov. 17, 1962.
90. *Europäische Wirtschaftsgemeinschaft,* Kommission, July, 1962.
91. *Ibid.,* Oct. 24, 1962, Brussels.
92. *Activity Program,* p. 63.
93. See Report on these events in *Die Welt,* Nov. 23, 1962.
94. The West German newspaper *Die Welt,* Feb. 15, 1964, published an interview with Professor Hallstein, High Commissioner, which concentrated on the political aspects of the EEG.
95. *Die Welt,* Nov. 24, 1963.

VI. Preliminary Appraisal

1. W. W. Rostow, *The Stages of Economic Growth* (Cambridge, 1960), deutsch Göttingen.
2. Quoted from a classified paper circulated within a German business association.
3. T. C. Koopmans, *Three Essays on the State of Economic Science* (New York, Toronto, and London, 1957), p. 206.
4. See note 2 above.
5. See note 37, Chap. IV.
6. Reported in *Die Welt,* Aug. 7, 1964.
7. Foreword to *Planung ohne Planwirtschaft.*

Bibliography

Albrecht, K. *Planifikateure beim Werk, Wirtschaft zwischen Zwang und Freiheit.* Düsseldorf, 1964.

Allemann, F. *Bonn ist nicht Weimar.* Cologne, 1956.

Altmann, R. "*Zur Rechtsstellung der öffentlichen Verbände,*" *Zeitschrift für Politik,* Bd. II (1955).

Arbeitsgemeinschaft deutscher wirtschaftswissenschaftlicher Forschungsinstitut, Langfristige Programmierung innerhalb der Marktwirtschaft (Report on part of the twenty-sixth Convention on June 21 and 22, 1963). Berlin, 1963. Published as *Beiheft* no. 10 *der Konjunkturpolitik.*

Arendt, Hannah. *Vita Activa toder Vom tätigen Leben.* Stuttgart, 1960.

————. *The Origins of Totalitarianism.* New York, 1951.

Bickel, W. in *Finanz- und währungspolitische Bedingungen stetigen Wirtschaftswachstums, Schriften des Vereins für Sozialpolitik.* No. 15. Berlin and Munich, 1959.

Bloch-Lainé, F. *Pour une réforme de l'entreprise.* Paris, 1963.

Blum, L. "*Der Grüne Bericht 1964,*" *Die Aussprache,* ed. *Arbeitsgemeinschaft selbständiger Unternehmer* (March 3, 1964).

Bouton, A. *La Fin des Rentiers, Histoire des fortunes privées en France depuis 1914.* Paris, 1932.

Breitling, R. *Die Verbände in der Bundesrepublik.* Meisenheim/Glan, 1955.

Clark, Colin. *The Conditions of Economic Progress.* 3rd ed. London, 1957.

Dahl, R. A. "Hierarchy, Democracy, and Bargaining in Politics and Economics," *Research Frontiers in Politics and Government.* Washington, D.C., 1955.

Dechamps, B. *Macht und Arbeit der Ausschüsse.* Meisenheim/Glan, 1954.

Deutscher Gewerkschaftsbund, Die Autonomie der Gewerkschaften in einem integrierten Europa, public. 12th European Convention of the Central Federation of German Labor (DGB). Düsseldorf, 1964.

————. *Sachverstand und Politik in der Demokratie,* ed., Düsseldorf, 1962.

Deutsches Industrie-Institut, *Der 17. September unter der Lupe,* Köln 1961, aus der Schriftenreihe: *Material zum Zeitgeschehen,* Nr. 10, 1961.

————. *Prognosen als Grundlage der Wirtschaftspolitik, Beiträge des Deutschen Industrie-Instituts,* Nr. 1, 1964.

Dungern, F. von *"Die drei Theorien vom Staatshaushalt," Zeitschrift für die gesamte Staatswissenschaft* (Bd. 108, 1952).

Ellis, H. S. "The Rediscovery of Money," *Money, Trade and Economic Growth* (in honor of J. W. Williams). New York, 1951.

Erbe, René. *Die national-sozialistische Wirtschaftspolitik 1933–1939 im Lichte der modernen Theorie.* Zurich, 1958.

Erhard, Ludwig. *Wohstand für Alle.* Düsseldorf, 1957.

Eschenburg, Th. *Herrschaft der Verbände.* Stuttgart, 1955.

Eucken, W. *Die Grundlagen der Nationalökonomie* 1st ed. Jena, 1940.

————. *Grundsätze der Wirtschaftspolitik,* posthumous ed. Hamburg, 1959.

————. *Die Wettbewerbsordnung und ihre Verwirklichung, ORDO,* Bd. 2. Bad Godesberg, 1949.

Fischer, H. *Marketing. Stuttgart,* 1959.

Fischer, M. *Unternehmer zur Führung berufen.* Düsseldorf, 1963.

Fischer, Ruth. *Stalin und der deutsche Kommunismus.* Frankfurt/M., 1950.

Flender, A. *Die Verantwortung des Unternehmers.* Bonn, 1961.

Föhl, C. *Geldschöpfung und Wirtschaftskreislauf.* Munich and Leipzig, 1937.

Forsthoff, E. *Lehrbuch des Verwaltungsrechts,* 7th ed. Munich and Berlin, 1958.

————. *Über Massnahmegesetze, in Forschungen und Berichte aus dem öffentlichen Recht, Jellinek-Gedächtnisschrift.* Munich, 1955.

Friedrich, C. J. "The Continental Tradition of Training Administrators in Law and Jurisprudence," *Journal of Modern History,* Vol. XI, No. 2 (1939).

————, and Z. K. Brzezinski. *Totalitarian Dictatorship and Autocracy.* Cambridge, 1956.

Friedrich-Ebert-Stiftung. *Nationalbudget und Wirtschaftspolitik.* Hanover, 1962.

————. *Planung in der Marktwirtschaft.* Stuttgart, 1964.

Gehlen, A. *"Soziologische Aspekte des Eigentumsproblems in der Industrie-Gesellschaft,"* in *Eigentum und Eigentümer, Veröffentli-*

chungen der Walter-Raymond-Stiftung. Cologne and Opladen, 1960.

————.*Die Seele im technischen Zeitalter.* Hamburg, 1947.

Gleske L. *Die Liquidität in der Kreditwirtschaft.* Frankfurt/M, 1953.

Götz, H. H. *Weil alle besser leben wollen, Portrait der deutschen Wirtschaftspolitik.* Düsseldorf, 1963.

Granick, D. *The European Executive.* New York, 1962.

Gross, H. *Unternehmer in der Politik.* Düsseldorf, 1954.

Habermas, J. *Strukturwandel der Öffentlichkeit.* Neuwied, 1962.

Hallgarten, G. W. F. *Hitler, Reichswehr und Industrie.* Frankfurt/M., 1962.

Halm, G. N. *Geld, Aussenhandel und Beschäftigung.* 3rd ed., trans. Munich, 1957.

Hansmeyer, K.-H. *Der Weg zum Wohlfahrtsstaat.* Frankfurt/M., 1957.

Harmening and Duden. *Die Währungsgesetze.* Munich and Berlin, 1949, Supplement 1950.

Hayek, F. *The Road to Serfdom,* German trans. Erlenb./Zurich, 1945 *Marktwirtschaft und Wirtschaftspolitik, ORDO,* Bd. 6. Bad Godesberg, 1954.

Hirsch-Weber, Wolfgang, ed. *Gewerkschaften im Staat.* Düsseldorf, 1955.

Hiss, D. *Kosten und Preise in der Bundesrepublik 1950 bis 1960.* Berlin, 1963.

Hofer, Walther, ed. and comment. of *Der Nationalsozialismus, Dokumente 1933–1945.* Fischer Books, Frankfurt/M., 1957.

Huber, E. R. *Wirtschaftsverwaltungsrecht,* Bd. II. Tübingen, 1954.

Irmler, H. Review of Hayek, *The Road to Serfdom,* in *ORDO,* Bd. 2. Bad Godesberg, 1949.

Jahn, H.-D. *Gesellschaft und Demokratie in der Zeitwende.* 2nd ed. Cologne, 1955.

Jeidels. *Das Verhältnis der Grossbanken zur Industrie.* Leipzig, 1905.

Jouvenel, B. de. *De la Souveraineté, à la recherche du bien politique.* Paris, 1955.

Kaiser, J. H. (ed.), *Planungi,* Baden-Baden, 1965.

Keynes, John M. *Allgemeine Theorie der Beschäftigung, des Zinses und des Geldes.* German ed., Berlin, 1955, 1st ed. 1936.

Kirchheimer, O. *"Vom Wandel der politischen Opposition,"* Archiv für Rechts- und Sozialphilosophie (1957), XLIII/1.

Konzentration in der Wirtschaft, Bericht über das Ergebnis einer Untersuchung der Konzentration in der Wirtschaft (February 29, 1964), Bundestag-Drucksache, IV/2320. 4- Wahlperiode, S. 48.

Koopmans, T. C. *Three Essays on the State of Economic Science.* New York, Toronto, and London, 1957.

Lange, M. G., G. Schulz, K. Schutz *et al. Parteien in der Bundesrepublik, Schriften des Instituts für Politische Wissenschaften* Berlin, Stuttgart, and Düsseldorf, 1955.

List-Gesellschaft. *Planung ohne Planwirtschaft,* Basel and Tübingen, 1964, ed. by A. Plitzko.

Lochner, Louis P. *Tycoons and Tyrant: German Industry from Hitler to Adenauer.* Chicago, 1954.

Lüke, R. E. *Von der Stabilisierung zur Krise,* Ed. Basle Center for Economic and Financial Research, Ser. B., Nr. 3. Zurich, 1958.

Lutz, F. A. *Das Grundproblem der Geldverfassung.* Stuttgart and Berlin, 1936.

———. *Geldpolitik und Wirtschaftsordnung, ORDO.* Bad Godesberg, Bd. 2, 1949.

McKenzie, R. T. *British Political Parties.* Melbourne, London, and Toronto, 1955.

Mangoldt, H. von. *Das Bonner Grundgesetz.* Berlin and Frankfurt, 1953.

Marcuse, Ludwig. *Mein Zwanzigstes Jahrhundert.* Munich, 1960.

Meimberg, R. *Einige Grundfagen der Geldpolitik und Notenbankverfassung in Jahrbuch für Nationalökonomie und Statistik 169,* 1957.

Meinhold, H. *Aspekte einer europäischen Programmierung,* ed. by the Association of Chemical Industries, Heft 5, 1963.

Miksch, L. *Die Geldschöpfung in der Gleichgewichtstheorie, ORDO,* Bd. 2. Bad Godesberg, 1949.

Mises, L. von. *Theorie des Geldes und der Umlaufsmittel.* Munich and Leipzig, 1912.

Mohler, Armin. *Die konservative Revolution in Deutschland 1918–1932.* Stuttgart, 1950.

Morgenstern, O. *Die Grenzen der Wirtschaftspolitik.* Vienna, 1934.

Mühlen, Norbert. *Der Zauberer, Leben und Anleihen des Dr. H. H. G. Schacht.* Zurich, 1938.

Müller-Armack, A. *Wirtschaftslenkung und Marktwirtschaft.* Hamburg, 1948.

Muthesius, V. *Inflation.* Frankfurt/M., 1958.

Naphtali, Fritz. *Wirtschaftsdemokratie, ihr Wesen, Weg und Ziel, Hrsg. im Auftrag des Allgemeinen Deutschen Gewerkschaftsbundes.* Berlin, 1928.

Nöll von der Nahmer, Robert. *Der volkswirtschaftliche Kreditfonds.* Berlin, 1934.

――――. *Vom Werden des neuen Zeitalters.* Heidelberg, 1957.

Nolte, Ernst. *Der Faschismus in seiner Epoche.* Munich, 1963.

OEEC. *Europas Energiebedarf, sein Anwachsen, seine Deckung, Bericht einer Sachverständigengruppe,* ed. *Bundesministerium für wirtschaftliche Zusammenarbeit.* Bonn, 1956.

Ortlieb, H.-D., ed., *Wirtschaftsordnung und Wirtschaftspolitik ohne Dogma.* Hamburg, 1954.

Parteienrechts-Kommission. Bericht der vom Bundesinnenminister eingesetzten Parteienrechts-Kommission, Rechtliche Ordnung des Parteiwesens. Frankfurt/M., 1957.

Plenge, J. *Von der Diskontpolitik zur Herrschaft über den Geldmarkt.* Berlin, 1913.

Popitz, H., H. P. Bahrdt, H. Kesting, and E. A. Jüres. *Technik und Industriearbeit.* Tübingen, 1957.

――――. *Das Gesellschaftsbild des Arbeiters.* Tübingen, 1957.

Raspini, Heinz. *Wirtschaftspolitik und Friede, in Werkhefte,* 17 Jgg., Heft 12 (Dec. 1963), Munich.

Riesman, David, *et al. The Lonely Crowd.* New Haven, 1950.

Roche, Emile. *L'Or n'est plus Roi.* Paris, 1942.

Röpke, W. *"Wirtschaftssystem und internationale Ordnung, Prolegomena," ORDO,* Bd. 4, Bad Godesberg, 1951.

Rostow, W. W. *The Stages of Economic Growth.* Cambridge, 1960, German ed., Göttingen.

Rüstow, A. *"Die staatspolitischen Voraussetzungen des wirtschaftspolitischen Liberalismus," Der Deutsche Volkswirt,* Jg. 7, Nr. 6 (Berlin, 1932).

――――. *Ortsbestimmung der Gegenwart,* Erlenbach/Zurich, 1950, 1952, and 1957.

Saint-Jean, Maurice de. *La Politique économique et financière du Troisième Reich, L'Oeuvre du Docteur Schacht.* Paris, 1936.

Schacht, H. G. *"Währung und Wirtschaft"* (paper read at Düsseldorf, Jan. 8, 1925, printed).

――――. *Die Stabilisierung der Mark.* Stuttgart, Berlin, and Leipzig, 1927.

――――. *Grundsätze deutscher Wirtschaftspolitik.* Oldenburg, 1932.

――――. *76 Jahre meines Lebens.* Bad Wörishofen, 1953.

Schapiro, Leonhard. *Die Geschichte der kommunistichen Partei der Sowjetunion.* German ed., Frankfurt/M., 1961.

Schelsky, H. *Wandlungen der deutschen Familie in der Gegenwart, Darstellung und Deutung einer empirisch-soziologischen Tatbestandsaufnahme.* Dortmund, 1953. rev. ed., Stuttgart, 1955.

――――. *Einsamkeit und Freiheit, Idee und Gestalt der deutschen Uni-*

versität und ihrer Reformen. Hamburg, 1963, *Rowohlts Deutsche Ezyklopädie.*

————. ed., et al., *Arbeiterjugend gestern und heute.* Heidelberg, 1955.

Schiller, Karl. *Sozialismus und Wettbewerb.* Hamburg, 1955.

Schmölders, G. *Finanzpolitik.* Berlin, 1955.

————. *Die Politiker und die Währung* (Report on a demoscopic study of public opinion on financial and currency questions, conducted among members of the third Bundestag.) Frankfurt/M., 1959.

Schneider, E. *Einführung in die Wirtschaftstheorie.* Bd. III, Tübingen, 1957.

Schumpeter, A. *Theorie der wirtschaftlichen Entwicklung.* Munich, 1913.

Stackelberg, H. von *"Möglichkeiten und Grenzen der Wirtschaftslenkung," ORDO,* Bd. 2, Bad Godesberg, 1949.

Strickrodt, G. *Die Finanzordnung als Lebensbasis der arbeitsteiligen Wirtschaft, Vortrag Karlsruher Versicherungswoche* (April 29, 1955).

VdI. *Der Auftrag unserer Zeit an die Technik,* (Report of the Fourth International Convention of Engineers.) Munich, 1963.

Veit, O. *Die Verantwortung der Notenbank, Der Wert unseres Geldes.* Frankfurt/M., 1958.

Verein für Sozialpolitik. Die Konzentration in der Wirtschaft. Berlin, 1961.

Vereinigung der deutschen Staatsrechtslehrer, Der Plan als verwaltungsrechtliches Institut, Veröffentlichungen, Heft 18. Berlin, 1960.

Vocke, W. *Gesundes Geld,* 2nd ed. Frankfurt/M., 1956.

Voigt, Fritz, and Walter Weddingen. *Zur Theorie und Praxis der Mitbestimmung.* Berlin, 1962.

Walter-Raymond-Stiftung. Bd. 1: *Eigentum und Eigentümer in unserer Gesellschaftsordnung. Cologne and Opladen,* 1960; Bd. 4: *Die unternehmerische Verantwortung in unserer Gesellschaftsordnung.* Cologne and Opladen, 1964.

Weber, Alfred. *Prinzipien der Geschichts- und Kultursoziologie.* Munich, 1951.

Weber, W. *Spannungen und Kräfte im westdeutschen Verfassungssystem.* Stuttgart, 1951.

Wirtschaftswissenschaftliches Institut des Deutschen Gewerkschaftsbundes. Notenbank im Umbau. Cologne, 1951.

Zahn, E. *Soziologie der Prosperität.* Cologne, Berlin, 1960.

Zangen, W. *Die Praxis der industriellen Unternehmensführung.* 2nd ed. Essen, 1962.

Zapf, W. (ed.), *Beitrage zur Analyse der deutschen Oberschicht* (Munich, 1965).

Index

Act of Allocation of Housing (1953), 20
Adenauer, Konrad, 83, 115; Weimar tradition and, 66; "Federal Lists," 68; clash with Central Bank, 139n
Agartz, Victor, 123
AGPLAN (*Arbeitsgemeinschaft Planungsrechnung*), 71
Agriculture, planning, 76
Allied intervention, 11; economic, 9; military, 9; political, 9
Anticartel Act: exemptions, 23; ineffective, 37; limits cooperative planning, 72

Banking: concentration process, 74; influence on planning, 74; aid to macroeconomic planning, 74–75. *See also* Central Bank
Bonn Parliament, 65–70 *passim;* policy position, 70; economic order, 70
Brenner, Otto, 62
Budget: lack of state, 28; factors in public, 28; influence of, 103; proposal, 104; and *planstellen,* 104
Bundestag: postwar membership in, 66; Weimar heritage, 66; response to postwar conditions, 67; reliance on experts, 67. *See also* Bonn Parliament
Businessmen, 70

Cartels: coal and potash, 2; restrictions on, 14; postwar, 76; under state supervision, 76; administered by state, 76
Catholic Center party, 3
Central Bank: history of, 94; op-poses planning, 94; opposes "other planning," 95; inflation control, 95; macroeconomic concern, 96
Christian Democratic party: support Erhard, 136n
Christian Union (CGD), 60
Civil servants: major executive function, 47
Clark, Colin, 48
Clay, General Lucius D., 12
Coal and steel, 76; nationalization of, 145–46n; rationalization organization of, 145–46n
Coal and Steel Community, 15, 73
Coal industry: cartel nature of, 76
Codetermination Act of 1951, 23, 61, 122; defined, 55
Collective bargaining: safeguarded, 2; general import of, 80; after World War II, 81; role of experts in, 81–82; attempts at formalizing, 82; complex, 84; labor uneasy about, 84; management uneasy about, 84
Commercialism: check on liberal planning, 44
Commissariat au Plan, 18
Common Market. *See* European Economic Community
Communism: German experience incompatible with Russian guidelines, 2
Competition: role in budget, 28
Compromise: factors in budget, 28; role in Liberalist politics, 44
Compulsory arbitration, 4. *See also* Weimar Republic *and* Collective bargaining
Conflict: factor in budget, 28

157

158   WEST GERMANY

"Constitution of Enterprises" Law (1952), 23

Construction Curtailment Act of 1962, 24

Consulting service: significance to macroeconomic analysis, 89–90

Consumers cooperatives: cooperate with labor unions, 79

Control devices: and cyclical changes, 31

Cooperation: extent of between firms, 72–73; in coal and steel industries, 73

Coordination: lack of between governmental levels, 26; instances of inconsistency, 26, 27; lack of, 108–11

Currency reform: of 1923–24, 3; result in period of normalcy, 3; postwar, 11; opposition to, 12, 14, 141n

Deficit: during Great Depression, 4

Denationalization, 15

Deutsche Angestellton Gewerkshaft (DAG), 60

Deutsche Demokratische Republik (DDR). See East Germany

Deutsche Wirtschaftswunder, 15, 16. See also German economic miracle

Devaluation: of the mark, 11

Discrimination: against Jews, 6; of foreign currency, 21; against smaller enterprises, 139n

Disequilibrium: forces responsible for, 37, 38

East Germany, 1; economic growth compared to West Germany, 17

Economic analysis: problem within West Germany, 38

Economic associations: outside legal framework, 84; private, 85; defined, 85; as collective organizations, 85; aims, 86; macroeconomic implications, 86

Economic goals: post-World War II, 9

Economic Parliament: ineffective, 2

Economic policy: linked with parliamentary democracy, 8; use system theories as models, 33; derived from old ideas, 41; inconsistent with old concepts, 41–42; linked more closely to politics, 42; finds support in legislature, 43; no differentiation from social policy, 46

Economic Report (1964), 109–11

Economy: deliberalization of, 7

Enterprises: ownership of competitive, 92

Erhard, Ludwig, 12, 65; and Soziale Marktwirtschaft, 13; influenced by Freiburg school of economics, 13; "Erhard's system," 18; on reallocation, 25; on economic inconsistency, 41; people's capitalism and, 49; and European Economic Community, 113; conflict with Hallstein, 114; and Christian Democrats, 136n

Eucken, Walter, 33; designer of neo-liberalism, 35; on competition, 37; head of Freiburg school, 136n

European Economic Community, 15, 65; character of plan, 113; High Commission, 113–14; programs, 114; bureaucratic penetration difficult, 114

Experts: necessary, 100; dual role of, 100; dilemmas encountered in role fulfillment, 100. See also Generalists

Extraordinary Federated Congress of 1963, 78; press for macroeconomic planning, 78

Family Allowance Act (1954), 21

Farmers' League (Bauernverband), 59

Feder, Gottfried, 7

Federal Economic Council: proposed, 101; membership, 101; duties, 101; purposes, 101

Federal Expellee Act (1953), 20

Federal subsidies: direct and indirect, 22

Federation of German Industries